## Direct Encounters

*It may be impossible to prove definitively that these men and women were abducted by UFOs, but lie detectors and hypnosis have produced no alternative explanations . . .*

As the authors say: 'What is important is that these people sincerely believe that their abductions were real events, and they live their lives accordingly. No amount of family, community, media, or government pressure has made them back down. They are all the more impressive in that their belief that the capture was a real event has changed their lives in ways we never expected to find when we began the project. Not all of us would have the fortitude to stand up and be counted as an abductee and continue to stand alone no matter how rough the voyage became.'

Judith M. Gansberg is author of STALAG USA and the award-winning writer of TV documentary films. Alan L. Gansberg is editor of several entertainment periodicals and he has written feature articles and reviews for the *New York Times*.

# Direct Encounters

UFO Abductees Tell Their Own Story.

---

# Judith M. Gansberg and Alan L. Gansberg

**CORONET BOOKS**
Hodder and Stoughton

Copyright © 1980 by Judith M.
Gansberg and Alan L. Gansberg

First published by Walker Publishing Co. Inc. 1980

*Coronet Edition 1981*

**British Library C.I.P.**

Gansberg, Judith M.
  Direct encounters.
  1. Unidentified Flying objects – Sightings and encounters – United States
  I. Title  II. Gansberg, Alan L.
  0019'42'0973  TL789.3

ISBN 0 340 26685 6

---

This book is sold subject to the condition that
it shall not, by way of trade or otherwise, be
lent, re-sold, hired out or otherwise circulated
without the publisher's prior consent in any
form of binding or cover other than that in
which this is published and without a similar
condition including this condition being
imposed on the subsequent purchaser.

Printed and bound in Great Britain for
Hodder and Stoughton Paperbacks, a
division of Hodder and Stoughton Ltd.,
Mill Road, Dunton Green, Sevenoaks,
Kent (Editorial Office: 47 Bedford
Square, London, WC1 3DP) by
Cox & Wyman Ltd.,
Cardiff Road, Reading.

# Contents

| | | |
|---|---|---|
| | *Acknowledgments* | *page* vi |
| | *Introduction* | vii |
| 1 | Direct Encounters | 11 |
| | *Barney and Betty Hill* | 17 |
| | *Carl Higdon* | 21 |
| | *Louise Smith, Mona Stafford, and Elaine Thomas* | 24 |
| | *Travis Walton* | 28 |
| | *Lydia Stalnaker* | 31 |
| | *Charles Hickson and Calvin Parker* | 35 |
| | *Ellecia Gruen* | 37 |
| | *Jeffrey Greenhaw* | 39 |
| | *Jessica Rolfe* | 41 |
| 2 | What the Record Shows | 50 |
| 3 | What Will the Neighbors Say? | 66 |
| 4 | Family Loyalty | 85 |
| 5 | You Read It Where? | 98 |
| 6 | Official Cover-Up | 116 |
| 7 | Suddenly Aware | 135 |
| 8 | Heavenly Messenger | 154 |
| 9 | Where Are They Today? | 171 |
| | *Conclusion* | 185 |
| | *Bibliography* | 189 |

# Acknowledgments

This book would never have come into being without the assistance and help of many gracious individuals.

We owe a special thanks to Lewis R. Chambers, who introduced us to the material, and to Harry Lebelson, who got us started in the research.

This book could never have been written without the cooperation of Betty Hill, Mona Stafford, Louise Smith, Travis Walton, Carl Higdon, Charles Hickson, Lydia Stalnaker, Ellecia Gruen, Jeffrey Greenhaw, and Jessica Rolfe. We owe them a debt of gratitude.

We are equally grateful to Dr. James Harder, Dr. R. Leo Sprinkle, and Dr. Iris H. Maack for sharing their files and their very valuable time with us and to our father, Martin Gansberg, who was our most severe critic in the preparation of this manuscript.

We would also like to acknowledge most thankfully the following people for helping us locate witnesses and information: Mrs. Mary Kellett, Edward Witt, Darlis Clark, Coral Lorenzen, Rosetta Holmes, Dr. Julian Bosco, Barney Mathis, Michael Rogers, Allan Morris, and Clyde Walker; and the following for acting as a sounding board for our ideas: Dr. Tom Wallach, Donald Freed, and Judy's husband, Bob Burger.

We must credit our mother, Agatha Gansberg, for suggesting the title *Direct Encounters* and give a tummy rub but no thanks to Margaret Althea de Revoix (Maggie), the golden retriever who seemed determined to distract us from completing this manuscript.

J.M.G.
A.L.G.
STAMFORD, CT. 1979

# Introduction

Unidentified flying objects (UFOs) are a worldwide phenomenon. In Italy, there are nine publications devoted to reporting celestial sightings, more than on documented scientific achievement. The Politburo of the Soviet Union has become so curious about the frequency of such visions in their country that a government bureau for UFO study has been created.

The United States is not immune. A 1973 Gallup poll revealed that more than half of the American public believed UFOs were real, not imaginary. UFO scholars claim that since World War II there have been close to 20 million sightings in that country alone.

Scientists agree that it is possible, even probable, that there are other humanoid races in the universe. The National Aeronautical and Space Administration (NASA) feels that the odds are so great for finding other intelligent beings that it placed a message aboard the Pioneer 10 spacecraft that swung past Jupiter into outer space in 1973.

The message was in the form of a pictorial plaque aimed at being interpreted by another race that might intercept it. On the plaque were sketches of a man and woman, the planetary map of our solar system, a code based on the position of fourteen pulsating neutron stars pointing out our sun, and another code, based on the wavelength of hydrogen, which gives the size of the human figures. The man's hand is raised in a gesture of greeting or good will.

## DIRECT ENCOUNTERS

Astronomers have been trying to send messages to other races on faraway planets since the 1920s. Norwegian, French, Dutch, Russian, English, and American observatories have been sending out radio signals and picking up later readings of signals returning to earth. Some of the radio impulses have been echoes of the original messages, but others, arriving after periods of delay, cannot be identified. Could they be answers from other worlds?

In 1972, Professor Vesvolod Troitsky of the Gorsky Observatory in Russia told a group of American reporters that he believed other civilizations were receiving and answering our signals but that this could not be confirmed, given the weakness of the signals and our technology. However, he conjectured, 'the first confirmed contact could come as early as a year from now.'

Many people are convinced that alien races are making contact with us, or at least some of us. Reports of encounters with humanoids traveling in unusual flying vehicles come from all over the world. At least 150 cases of people who claim to have been abducted have been studied and 'verified' by researchers in the United States.

This book is a compilation of the stories of the small percentage of these abductees who are willing to share their experiences with the public.

When we first began researching the material, we had no idea what these people who claim to have been abducted by extraterrestrial beings would be like. We wondered if they would be eccentric or 'normal,' whether they would try to persuade us with their evidence or be much more casual. We had first-hand knowledge of only one 'abductee,' Betty Hill, since we had seen her on a television talk show.

Frankly, at the outset we were skeptical. There are many differences in their stories, the solid proof is negligible, and the information we found in our initial research was often contradictory or, as we later discovered, incorrect. As we began to meet and interview the abductees, discuss the evidence with researchers, and read more about the cases, we

## INTRODUCTION

found that the subject was far more fascinating than we had imagined. The abductees are warm, open people with a good sense of humor about their lives and the aftermath of their encounters.

In this book, we have assembled the stories of their abductions, the effects they had on them and their families, the way the world has reacted to them, and how their view of the world has been changed.

Since we are probably the first to attempt interviewing such a large number of abductees and meshing their stories into one manuscript, we feel it is appropriate for us to tell the stories from their points of view. The individual experiences are related as introspective biographies. However, the perceptions of so many are represented that there are, of necessity, issues raised that do not pertain to all of them.

Dr. James Harder, professor of engineering at the University of California at Berkeley, a leading UFO researcher, told us that 'the person who investigates UFO abductions and comes to the conclusion that there are no real patterns is expressing a great deal of wisdom; finding a common denominator has been a great frustration.'

After our interviews with the abductees, we have no reason to disagree with Dr. Harder. There is no one piece of data that fits into all the stories. While there are some similarities, some overlappings from story to story, no one thing or perception has been realized by all of them. They did not all see the identical aliens or interact in the same way with their captors. Nor have they had the same experiences since the incident. Some have developed psychic powers, and some have not. Some have altered their perceptions of God and the Bible; others still react in the same way. The differences only serve to make the retelling of their combined stories more intriguing and, perhaps, perplexing.

It is not for us to judge whether or not the abductions actually occurred since there is no tangible evidence and even experts are baffled. What is important is that these people sincerely believe that their abductions were real events, and they live their lives accordingly. No amount of family, community, media, or government pressure has made them back down. They are all the more impressive in that their belief that the capture was a real event has changed their lives in ways we never expected to find when we began the project. Not all of us would have the fortitude to stand up and be counted as an abductee and continue to stand alone no matter how rough the voyage became.

Frankly, as collaborators, we disagree in our attitudes toward UFOs in general. Therefore, we are not presuming to offer our own theories, nor contradict theirs.

However, we did find all their stories tremendously absorbing, and we hope that our retelling is faithful to their perceptions and attitudes.

Chapter One

# Direct Encounters

For years, dreamers have fantasized about space travel, speculated about encounters with alien races, wondered about worlds beyond. If a poll were taken, even informally, it might very well reveal that a majority of Americans believe some sort of life on other planets is conceivable.

The evidence is there. Proteins and their amino acids – major building blocks for life as we know it – have been found in meteorites that have penetrated the earth's atmosphere. Voyager I's findings that there could be volcanic activity on Eos, one of Jupiter's moons, indicate that the satellite could support life forms and add to the speculation about other organisms on our galaxy.

Even if we accept the premise that some sort of life does exist elsewhere, it is not easy to substantiate the notion that there are intelligent life forms and beings in the universe with knowledge and technology superior to ours. More shattering to our egos is the possibility that these superior alien races are studying our planet and life cycles in the same thorough way we hope someday to visit Mars and Jupiter and beyond.

In the United States, there is a group of people who have become convinced beyond any doubt that we are being visited and studied by extraterrestrial humanoids. Their proof is something that on a primitive level we hold sacred: their own word. These people – call them abductees, witnesses, contactees – number more than 150, who claim to have been captured by or to have encountered alien races on our planet who do, indeed, travel in spacecraft labeled unidentified flying objects, UFOs in common practice.

An abduction by a UFO. The very thought sounds absurd to man. The very image of a person who claims to be an abductee is one of an eccentric or someone looking for attention in a neurotic way. As for extraterrestrial beings, they are actors, characters from drama and fiction. They could not possibly be real.

Or are they? The burden of proof seems to rest on the shoulders of the witnesses. That is natural since most of us have been taught never to accept information, especially unusual information, on face value. All of us are impressed with title and position, and if a person without special qualifications offers evidence that may challenge those in high places, it is our nature to expect him to be damn sure of what he is saying.

Still the abductees have not fabricated their stories; they are firm in the belief that what happened to them is real. Sometimes their task in proving the reality of their experiences is as difficult as a missionary proving monotheism to pagans, but the abductees do not attempt to proselytize. It is just that, like a god that cannot be felt, touched, and seen, the abductees are not able to give conclusive proof of their encounters. What evidence they offer must be accepted on face value alone.

Because of the problem of acceptance, only a small proportion of abductees – 10–15 percent – have allowed their experiences to be discussed publicly. The majority will cooperate with researchers, so elements of their stories do surface, but their privacy is protected.

It is important to remember that those who went public did not choose the role of a visionary in society, did not ask to be considered prophets or special in any way, and did not want to be celebrities. According to psychologists and conclusions reached after personal interviews, none of them exhibit an inordinate desire for public recognition and fame. They are only trying to relate information they think we have the right, and the need, to know.

Perhaps the first charge against any abductee by disbelievers is that he or she is a phony, a charlatan, a character who wants to be in the limelight. It is possible that some people with nothing but a tall tale have slipped through, but, essentially, researchers are satisfied with their accuracy and ability to weed out the fakers. The process of discovering that a person has encountered or has been abducted by aliens and having it confirmed by one of the major independent organizations that study UFOs is lengthy, especially since the memory of the contact is often sketchy, clouded by subconscious hysteria or amnesia.

UFO investigators work on several levels. The first group is made up of diverse personalities, from factory workers to physicists: people who are interested in the UFO phenomenon and can be trusted to do initial cursory questioning of witnesses.

After they have spoken to a witness and judged whether a story is worth following up, the investigators usually contact the independent UFO organization that they represent. There are more than a hundred groups in the world, many of which subscribe to the Intercontinental UFO Network (ICUFON). The most important of the independent groups in the United States are the Aerial Phenomena Research Organization (APRO), Center for UFO Studies (CUFOS), Mutual UFO Network (MUFON), National Investigations Committee on Aerial Phenomena (NICAP), Citizens Against UFO Secrecy, and Ground Saucer Watch (GSW).

Once assured by a group's local representative that the UFO witness is worth investigating further, one or more of these organizations will send in their 'big guns' to question the witness, perhaps even placing the abductee under hypnosis to extract further details. The researchers are frequently highly respected psychologists, professors, or engineers who have devoted much of their time to study in the field.

Three of the best-known and most skilled researchers agreed

to explain their methods and share their findings with us. Dr. James A. Harder, professor of engineering at the University of California at Berkeley, is director of research for APRO. He became involved in UFO research twenty-five years ago after stumbling upon a puzzling case in which several witnesses reported seeing the identical unknown craft. His scholarly publications and speaking engagements have brought him recognition among UFO enthusiasts within the scientific community as a leader in the field.

Dr. R. Leo Sprinkle, a psychologist who is director of counseling and testing and professor of counseling services at the University of Wyoming, Laramie, has been a devoted UFO researcher since he had a sighting of an unknown craft himself in 1950. He is a consultant to APRO, was a consultant to the Condon Commission UFO Project at the University of Colorado in 1968 and has written more then three dozen articles and scholarly papers on UFOs and related phenomena.

These two men have between them verified more than 100 abductions. Both are skilled in hypnotic techniques and indepth interviewing procedures.

Some abductees require more intensive psychological counseling to help them remember and cope with the details of their experience. Dr. Iris H. Maack, a psychologist operating from her private office in Savannah, Georgia, has worked with more than fifty verified abductees. She studied for her doctorate at Duke University. While a student there, she became intensely interested in parapsychology and later worked at the Foundation for Research on the Nature of Man, which is affiliated with Duke. The foundation is renowned for its advanced research into parapsychology (psychokinesis, extrasensory perception, and precognition).

Unlike Drs. Harder and Sprinkle, Dr. Maack does not investigate UFOs. Her research centers on her specialty: the psychological effects of an abduction and newly developed parapsychological abilities found in some abductees.

These experts explained to us that the first thing they do when meeting the alleged abductee is to have a relaxed conversation. They will discuss the person's life, what he thinks happened that day or night, how much he knows about UFOs, and so forth.

Most investigators have developed the instinct for picking out a phony. Usually, the individual trying to perpetrate a hoax first asks about publicity and the chance of making money from the story. If that is the case, the researcher bows out. On the other hand, if the abductee is obviously disturbed by what has happened, if there is a fearful reaction and a sincere interest in the subject and a multitude of questions about UFOs, the researcher can go ahead.

A lie-detector test, however degrading, is frequently employed as a means of determining further if the truth is being told. Often this is for the sake of the abductee, as neighbors and friends will usually react with greater kindness if the polygraph test shows the abductees are being honest. It is not unusual for the test to have been performed by local police or other officials before the researcher arrives on the scene.

If necessary, and if the person is interested, the abductee is placed under hypnosis to unblock time lapses. This can be dangerous, and several abductees have been rapidly removed from their trance when the questioning became too emotionally intense.

Basically, the object is to listen, to be honest with the abductees and talk to them.

The majority of abductions and encounters, it has been found, follow three umbrella patterns. In one instance, the individual recalls seeing a UFO, which he assumes to be more than an earthly craft, and then finds that there exists a long period of time for which he has no memory at all called a time block or time lapse. In these cases, a persistent feeling that something unusual or frightening has happened during the forgotten period of time leads the individual to seek help either in the form of a UFO researcher or psychologist or both.

In the second instance, the individual has almost full recall of the events of the encounter. He may remember both the craft and the aliens. If it is an abduction, he may recall the events on board the craft in detail.

In the third group, the encounter is a memory that returns to the individual perhaps twenty years after the actual event.

All these experiences seem equally valid. Multiple visits are not uncommon in all three categories.

Let us say you have a memory of seeing a UFO land in your back yard, and you are convinced you've either been abducted or are a contactee. Is this personal instinct infallible?

No, says Dr. Maack, who has a well-documented case of a woman who was convinced she was speaking to aliens, whom she called 'The Great White Brotherhood.' So taken by these voices was this woman that she divorced her husband, as her voices commanded, and unknowingly took up with a charlatan. Upon examination, Dr. Maack determined that the woman was suffering from a psychotic delusion. She was treated and is now living a normal life again. She has never been visited by extraterrestrials.

Who are the people who have passed the scrutiny of the researchers? Specifically, as Dr. Harder, the APRO researcher, tells us, 60 percent of them have only a high school education, 13 percent are college graduates, about 12 percent have graduate degrees, and almost 16 percent have been children whose education is not complete. Although rural women constitute 61 percent of the abductees, a wide spectrum of our inhabitants – from blue-collar workers to physicians, from college students to homeworkers – has been captured.

We have compiled case histories of witnesses who have achieved national renown and others who are relating their encounters for the first time. These people decided to step forward because they thought their courage in allowing their names to be used would help others who might be too timid to seek the aid of researchers.

Whatever the reason and whether one chooses to go public with a real name, an alias, or not at all, Dr. Maack asks all those who feel they have had an experience similar to these documented cases to come forward and seek help.

'It is much better to relieve the anxiety of not knowing what has happened,' she says. 'If your experience matches some of the more famous ones, you should seek help. We can make it easier for you to deal with your fears and questions. Or, there is always the possibility that you have the misguided notion that you have been abducted when something else entirely is going on in your head. If that is true, please seek help. Your problem must be treated.'

The following abduction biographies have passed the criteria sternly established by the UFO investigators. For the abductees, no other story but the one they have to tell is acceptable.

## BARNEY AND BETTY HILL

The most famous and the most often publicized abduction is that of Barney and Betty Hill, whose names have become synonymous with UFOs and what is sometimes called UFO-ology. Despite Barney's death in 1969, media response has resulted in the couple's becoming cult figures to believers. Their story was fully documented in the best-selling book *The Interrupted Journey* by John G. Fuller. An affable woman, Betty Hill still talks readily about the abduction today and is always gracious about granting interviews.

Their story begins in September 1961. Barney, who was working in the South Boston post office and was able to return to their home in Portsmouth, New Hampshire, only when he had days off, arrived unexpectedly one morning. Betty, then a social worker, also had some time off and was delighted when Barney suggested they drive to Niagara Falls and Montreal for a few days. It was a vacation both could use.

In their haste to be on their way, the Hills did not take enough cash for the trip, and in the early 1960s cash was essential to travel, as credit cards had not saturated our life styles. They packed quickly, leaving a bag of fertilizer Barney had bought in the trunk of the car. Their dachshund, Delsey, accompanied them.

The three-day trip was an enjoyable one, but when they predictably ran short of cash, the Hills realized they would have to make the trip from Montreal to Portsmouth in one night, September 19. They crossed the Canada-U.S. border as evening turned into night, reached Colebrook, on U.S. Route 3 in New Hampshire, around 10:00 P.M. and stopped for a light snack. Since they knew the roads fairly well, they expected to reach Portsmouth no later than 3:00 A.M. They had 190 miles to travel. The area around Colebrook, in the White Mountains, was deserted, as it usually is in September when the summer vacationers have departed and the snow has not yet fallen to attract skiers.

Down the highway from Colebrook, near Lancaster, Betty and Barney spied a strange craft in the clear, dark sky. The object, which they initially believed was an airplane, followed them along the road, sometimes clearly visible, sometimes hidden by mountains.

Somewhere along the road, near a point known as Indian Head, they heard a strange beeping noise from the trunk of their car. The craft was getting closer, and both Barney and Betty began to feel some panic. Barney stopped the car and walked into an open field carrying a pair of binoculars, hoping to get a better view. What he said he saw was an enormous disc with curved glass windows and a brilliant glowing white light. As the craft hovered many yards away, Barney felt the irresistible urge to investigate it more closely. As he walked toward the craft, he could see structured windows and five or six beings peering back toward him, apparently wearing some sort of uniform. Betty screamed at him for being a 'damn fool' to have wandered so close, and Barney came back to the automobile. They got in and were about to drive off when the beeping noise began again; this time their car vibrated as well. Then they felt very drowsy.

Their next conscious awareness was of driving down the road near Ashland, about thirty-five miles from where they had stopped to investigate the craft. The car was beeping again, and slowly the Hills came out of a trancelike state. They saw a sign that read 'Concord 17 miles' and for the first time realized where they were. They arrived in Portsmouth at 5:00 A.M., two hours later than they had anticipated. They had no memory of driving from the encounter site to Ashland, and they wondered what had transpired during the unaccountable two hours.

Betty was sure almost immediately that they had seen a UFO, but Barney did not wish to discuss it. He thought that perhaps they had seen a Russian surveillance craft that had penetrated American radar protection, but after discussing the subject with friends at nearby Pease Air Force Base, he found that explanation less than adequate. Barney could also not explain the pink dyelike substance on Betty's blue dress or the warts that had sprung up in a circular pattern on his stomach or the spots on the car that contained high degrees of radioactivity.

For two years, they did not know the full details of that night. It bothered both of them, affecting their health severely. Betty had headaches, several bouts with pneumonia, and disturbing dreams. Barney's ulcers and high blood pressure worsened.

In 1964, hoping to aid Barney's health, the Hills made arrangements to see Dr. Benjamin Simon, a prominent Boston psychiatrist. When the Hills explained that they were concerned about those two unaccountable hours, Dr. Simon decided to place them under hypnosis separately.

The story they told under hypnosis changed their lives, and some might say made them a part of history forever.

According to the Hills, as they came around a bend in the road, they found it blocked by the alien beings, who gently coaxed them into the craft they had seen. They described the aliens as about five feet in height, with gray skin, large slanted eyes – but not Oriental in slant – a small nose, and a slight slit where a mouth should be. The strangers, the Hills asserted, walked erect and had well-proportioned bodies and hands with either four or five fingers. Barney recalled seeing hair. Betty said she saw none because the things had caps on their heads. They also did not recall where their dog Delsey was at this time. The Hills said they were led to separate examination rooms on the craft, where one alien sat on a stool and the others watched the proceedings. The leader, they said, talked with them in English while they were on the craft.

The examinations were thorough, the Hills said. Their bodies were poked and explored from their heads to their fingers to their genitals. Most of it was painless, but Betty remembered an excruciatingly painful probe being inserted into her navel, and Barney recalled a cup being placed on his abdomen, at the spot where he eventually contracted warts.

Betty had a lengthy discourse with the leader, who asked her questions about human age and life cycles and what food we eat. They appeared to have no concept of age, time, the earth year, or the types of foods she mentioned. Even the color yellow was unknown to them. Betty tried to explain our habits the best she could. The leader showed Betty a map of their solar system and trade routes, which she later recreated under hypnosis. (Experts who saw the map afterward had no knowledge of it. In 1972, after discovering a few more stars, a team of astronomers concluded that the map was of a Reticuli star system and wondered how Betty was able to place stars on the map that they had no knowledge of in the mid-1960s.) The aliens were also at first willing to give Betty a book to prove she had had this experience. She looked it over carefully and noticed they wrote from top to bottom of a page, similar to the Japanese or Chinese.

Immediately following this exchange, the aliens became very excited, the Hills said. They had discovered that Barney's teeth were removable while Betty's were not. They had no concept of dentures and did not understand when Betty tried to explain once more. The leader then decided to take the book back from Betty and told them they would have no recollection of the abduction after they left the craft.

In parting, the leader told Betty that if they wanted to see her again, they would know how to find her.

For years after the result of the hypnosis became public, the Hills agreed to appear on radio and television talk shows to discuss their experience. Betty still is convinced that the aliens' choice of them was a random one; nevertheless, it took many months for the Hills to fully accept the capture as a reality. For some time, they wanted to believe alternate theories of the lost two hours, that they had a psychotic delusion or a shared dream experience. None seemed satisfactory. Betty explains today: 'We knew we had seen a craft, a solid metal object. There was no escaping that. No other explanation besides an abduction fits as we remembered it.'

## Carl Higdon

Carl Higdon is described by those who know him as an honest, hard-working individual. Monday to Friday, he puts in a very long day, driving from his home in Rawlins, in south-central Wyoming, to Casper, about a hundred miles away, where he runs an oil service rig. On weekends and days off, he is most likely to be found hunting, antelope, deer, or elk, depending on the season. Texas born, he likes the life in Wyoming. He is fond of the area around Rawlins, a sparsely populated region with mountains to the north and west, flatlands to the east, and timberland to the south.

It was into this timberland, more specifically, the Medicine Bow National Forest, about forty miles south of Rawlins, that he eagerly drove, anticipating a few days of good elk hunting. It was October 25, 1974, and the air was cool, but not cold. By 4:00 P.M. Higdon realized this would not be his most lucky of days since he had yet to bag an elk despite having shot at five of them and found he had crossed into an area of the forest that other hunters rarely use. The region has much thicker vegetation than the rest of the woodlands, with only one road for vehicles to enter. Higdon had heard that 'weird things happen' in this part of the forest, but he had never put much stock in it.

He spied another elk within range, he lifted up his new 7-mm magnum rifle and pulled the trigger. The bullet burst out of the barrel, as it should, but after traveling fifty feet, its momentum just died, and it fell to the ground.

'I was kind of puzzled, but not scared or anything.' Higdon explains today. 'I walked out and picked up the bullet and put it in my pouch. I paused for a second, trying to figure out why this had happened, and I turned around to find this guy was standing there.'

That was the last thing Higdon remembered before 6:30 P.M., when he found himself several miles away. After walking a few yards, he located his pickup truck stuck in a ditch. He reached into the truck, grabbed the radio, and called for help. he told the sheriff that the truck was three miles from where he had left it, and now it was unexplainably in a mud hole as well. The sheriff asked him why anyone would drive a two-wheel-drive pickup into this terrain; it seemed ludicrous since four-wheel-drive vehicles had been known to get stuck there.

It was after 11:30 P.M. when they pulled the truck out of the mud. Higdon was dazed and confused, with various bruises on his body and a general feeling of aches and pains. He could not recognize his wife, Margery, who had arrived on the scene. He was taken to a nearby hospital for observation and remained there until Monday morning when his confusion subsided and he regained full consciousness.

Unlike many other abductees, Higdon had nearly complete recollection of his experience even before he was placed under hypnosis by Dr. R. Leo Sprinkle, the psychologist at the University of Wyoming. In fact, a detailed account of his abduction was published in a local newspaper on Tuesday, October 29, by which time his memory of the events of the abduction was quite clear and his amnesia had disappeared.

On November 17, Higdon was placed under hypnosis in his Rawlins home. A rugged forty-year-old man of better than average intelligence, he was considered a good subject for hypnosis. His memory seemed incisive.

As questions were asked, the particulars of the experience were revealed.

Higdon told Dr. Sprinkle and the other witnesses to the hypnosis that when he turned around after picking up the bullet, there had been two alien beings standing in the shade, neither resembling any human or creature he had ever seen on earth. Since Higdon does not drink, Dr. Sprinkle knew this was not an alcohol-induced apparition. The figures were six feet two inches to six feet four inches in height, with high-yellow skin and straw-colored hair that looked like a wheat field filled with stalk stubs, each about eight inches long. The strangers weighed about 180 pounds; instead of hands, they had conical stubs, appearing something like the bottom of an ice cream cone. They wore heavy space suits with a large star on the belt buckle.

Higdon said he stood motionless as one of the aliens floated a packet of pills toward him and instructed him to swallow one of the five capsules in the packet. He complied and found himself 'floating' toward a transparent spacecraft, which, he says, 'you couldn't see in the daylight if it were in the air.' Although he could see through the spacecraft from the outside, once he was inside, he saw objects and walls black in color, which obscured an outside view. He was instructed to sit in one of the black high-bucket seats; he felt the craft taking off. He can recall seeing or sensing that his pickup truck was attached to the craft and dropped somewhere, but he isn't sure.

Higdon's memory of the subsequent events is vague. He believes that he was taken '163,000 light miles' away and placed inside a cubicle, about five feet wide and seven feet long, where a helmet with six wires running off it was placed on his head. A sheet that appeared to be cloth, about four feet by eight feet, came out of the wall and was placed next to his body. After they examined him through this sheet for a few minutes, Higdon recalled, the aliens announced that he 'was not what they wanted' and were going to return him to earth.

Although they did not tell Higdon why he was not 'qualified' for their purposes and what they were searching for, they did ask if he would give them his rifle since, he says, 'they considered it an example of a primitive weapon.' In the course of a limited conversation, they confided in him that they visited earth often but that the sun's rays burned them, making it imperative that they remain in the shade at all times when they leave their vehicle.

The short dialogue is the last recollection Higdon has about the aliens, and he can think of no other explanation besides an abduction for what happened to him from 4:00 to 6:30 P.M. He claims he never would have driven his pickup truck into that area of the forest because he knows it was not adequate to maneuver in the rough terrain.

In retrospect, Higdon is himself surprised that he swallowed the pills floated toward him, as he rarely uses drugs, even aspirin. As for his courage in cooperating with the aliens, he says, 'I always told my wife that if I ever saw creatures from a UFO, I would talk with them. I said that as soon as other stories started coming out about them.'

## Louise Smith, Mona Stafford, and Elaine Thomas

January 6, 1976, was Mona Stafford's birthday. A long-time resident of Liberty, Kentucky, she had not treated the day as a particularly special occasion and had spent it at home painting. She had made plans to visit her sister for dinner, and before driving to her sister's house, she pulled into a gas station where her seventeen-year-old son Greg was to work that evening. There she met Louise Smith, whom she had known casually. Smith had frequented Stafford's art store which Mona had closed a few months before. Smith asked Stafford to come to her house to help her with a dress she was making. Stafford agreed.

After they had finished working on the dress, Smith and

Stafford were sipping coffee and chatting when Elaine Thomas, a neighbor, dropped by. Stafford also knew Thomas, and the three women decided to drive to a restaurant in Stanford, about thirty miles away. Why Stafford decided to forego her expected visit to her sister's house is still a mystery, even to her.

The women had a pleasant, leisurely meal, after which they took out sketching pads and made a few drawings of their surroundings. All had made art a hobby, and they enjoyed discussing their work.

At 11:15 P.M., the women were heading back toward Liberty. A few miles outside of Stanford, Stafford noticed a huge, metallic-gray craft close by. The other women also saw the object and immediately assumed it was an airplane about to crash. As they got closer, they realized it was not an airplane. They described the craft as being the size of a football field, with a white-dome top, a row of red lights underneath, and three or four bright-yellow lights burning steadily. A bluish light appeared at the bottom. The women continued to drive along the road, keeping an eye on the craft.

About a quarter mile down the road, the inside of the car was brightened by a bluish light that came from behind them. The women had a feeling of panic and drove faster, reaching eighty-five miles per hour on the speedometer. Smith recalled that she tried to slow the car down but found that it was driving of its own volition. Stafford grabbed the steering wheel to aid her, but neither woman could control the automobile.

Their eyes began to water and burn, and each said that they experienced a stinging, unbearable headache. The last thing they recalled at the time was the feeling that some force was pulling the car backward and to the left. The engine had stalled, yet the car was moving extremely fast. Smith said that she glanced at her watch and noticed the hands were spinning around and around on their axis.

After what seemed like no time to them, the three women found that they were entering Hustonville, eight miles from where they had encountered the craft. It was after 1:00 A.M., yet they had no recollection of what had transpired for an hour and a half, the period from their encounter to the present.

Returning to Smith's house in Liberty, they still had a burning sensation in their eyes. Their skin had a scaly feeling, their knuckles were bright red, and there were blisters underneath the rings they wore. Despite the lateness of the hour, they told a neighbor what they had seen. He put them in separate rooms and asked them each to draw a picture of the craft. Although they had not had time to discuss their impressions among themselves, the three women drew almost the identical picture.

They knew that there was some memory, deep inside, of what had transpired in the midnight hour. During the next few months, they were hypnotized by specialists several times, and a detailed account of the abduction surfaced. Elaine Thomas has since died, but Louise Smith and Mona Stafford will never forget that night.

'The space ship took the car and all three of us up,' Mona Stafford says. 'The aliens separated us and I can remember leaving one ship and finding myself aboard another, with three floors, and there was a dome over me. I knew Lou and Elaine were somewhere, but I didn't know where. I was afraid I'd never see them again. The time seemed so long, even though it was only an hour and a half. Somehow, I also had the feeling I was in a cave or volcano – underground somewhere.'

'The aliens were about four to four-and-a-half feet tall,' Louise Smith picks up the story. 'They wore something like hoods over their heads and their bodies were covered. All that was visible were their frightening eyes, very dark ones, and their hands, which were like a bird wing would be if you could stretch it out. They were gray in color. I still can see those eyes. They were so large and pointed towards the temples.'

The women said they were subjected to a terribly painful examination. First, their arms were pinned down to tables, and warm, soft liquid was poured over their bodies, which formed a mold of their figures. While the liquid was on, they felt as if they would suffocate, and the aliens pulled it off with great force, as one might pull off a bandage. Then they twisted the women's arms and legs, as if they were experimenting with the stress human bones and muscles could endure before they snapped. Smith specifically remembers that her neck hurt throughout the examination, and all three women found they had red welts on their necks for several days after the abduction. Stafford further recalled that during her examination the aliens removed her eyeballs, looked them over, then returned them to her sockets.

In the separate rooms, their memories of which are sketchy, there was a computerlike terminal with sixteen flashing lights, which Smith remembers pulsated with the rhythm of her heart. At the time, she was convinced the machine was keeping her alive, that it was some sort of heart or life-sustaining monitor. They also said the rooms were very hot, another reason Stafford suspected they were inside a volcano.

Smith and Stafford can still not recall how or when they were released. They have been given polygraph tests, which could find no falsehoods in their statements. Both admit that the memory of the night still haunts them, and the capture and examination become more vivid each day. Their case is undoubtedly the best-known and most scrutinized group abduction.

Months after the original encounter, two of the women made an additional contact with the aliens, again not of their choosing.

Mona Stafford had been staying with her parents in an effort to adjust to life in the wake of her experience, but one evening she felt compelled to return to the mobile home where she lived. She turned on the radio and was relaxing on the couch when she heard a voice within her mind that told her to turn around. When she did, she said, she saw that one of the aliens, about five feet tall, was standing near her kitchen counter.

The being, bathed in a bright light, told her telepathically to look into his eyes. She refused, continuing to stare at his reddish-gold-colored hair and beard. The being ordered her to do it a second time, and she complied. 'There wasn't any point in fighting,' she says. 'I do remember that I tried to grab the phone, but a force wouldn't let me near it. I don't think I was frightened of him. I just don't recall having any thoughts at all.'

The humanoid, whom Stafford says 'looked the way they were described in Biblical days,' was dressed in a shiny robelike covering. She does not remember all the details of the encounter but remains perplexed about something that was said to her. 'I remember him saying, "Buree, the mind is still hungry,"' she explains. 'After he had disappeared I went over to my folks and looked up that word "Buree," but I couldn't find it anywhere. Dr. Sprinkle and the others who interviewed me couldn't identify it with any language. But that's what he said, "Buree, the mind is still hungry," and then he just vanished.'

After the unearthly being left, Stafford checked all the windows and doors and discovered, as she suspected, that they were locked. She then walked over to her parents' home.

'Dad said he opened the door and I just walked right past him in a daze,' she recalls. 'I went straight to the dictionary, and then Mom and I checked the Bible, too, looking for that word.'

Elaine Thomas had a later experience with the aliens, also, albeit much less startling than Stafford's. After Thomas returned to her home from the hospital several weeks before she died, she noticed that there would be a solitary brightly lit UFO in the sky nearby, waiting and watching daily. She would stare at it from time to time, also. On several occasions, it slowly approached the house and then returned to its observation point. She phoned Stafford to talk about it but never reported it to the authorities or the UFO investigators.

## Travis Walton

It was what he later described as 'November 5, 1975 – an ordinary sunny fall day,' but for Travis Walton the day would end in anything but the usual manner.

Travis, in his early twenties, was among a crew of seven men thinning the trees in the Apache-Sitgreaves National Forest in Arizona, near Heber and Snowflake in the eastern part of the state. The day had begun early, as is required for most outdoor work. By six o'clock, the sun was setting, and the seven tired men got back into their van to return home.

They drove a few miles, mostly in silence except for isolated jokes and maybe some tired groans. They were not looking for the unusual sight that suddenly was upon them; all seven men saw the same strange object. It was a large luminous craft hovering over some foliage, just yards from where their truck moved slowly on the road. They stopped the truck to get a closer look and noticed that this was, indeed, a strange sight. It seemed golden, emitting an eerie glow that appeared almost frightening against the deep, dark-blue sky. There appeared to be windowpanes on all sides of the fifteen- to twenty-foot craft, which seemed to be made of a silver-metallic material, but it had no visible openings. It looked like 'two pie pans placed lip to lip with a small bowl turned down on top,' they said.

For reasons he still does not understand, Walton felt compelled to get out of the truck and inspect the sight. Despite the pleas of his fellow workers, Walton approached the craft until he was struck by a bluish ray, knocking him to the ground, where he blacked out. The other men took off down the road, fearing for their own safety. When they returned to the site half an hour later, Walton was gone.

A five-day search revealed no clues to the whereabouts of the perhaps too curious Walton. Five days and six hours after the incident, Walton unexplainably opened his eyes at midnight and found that he was on the side of a road leading to Heber, thirty miles from the site of the abduction, with little or no memory of what had transpired.

Under hypnosis, Walton was able to recall about an hour of his experience, no more, before the severity of his emotions made the trance potentially dangerous to his health.

He recalled being unconscious in a room and awaking to

find himself surrounded by short, slim, chalk-white men. They had no hair, huge dark eyes with no eyelids, small facial features and small hands, and were wearing red jump suits with no visible openings or zippers and pink foot coverings. As they came toward him, he pushed one away and remembers that the alien felt as if he were made of marshmallows. The room had drab metallic-gray walls, a table on which he had been lying unconscious, and one light.

Later, he found himself in another room, which resembled a planetarium in shape but did not contain any astronomical markings. He wandered through this area, highly confused, when he came upon a six foot two inch human being; at least it appeared to be human at first glance. The man had blond-brown coarse hair, a deep, even golden tan, and no sign of a beard. He was well proportioned and wore a bright-blue space suit, black boots, and a helmet.

Although Walton repeatedly tried to communicate with this masculine-looking figure, he received no response. He was led down a ramp from the smaller craft into a large, dimly lit, humid area that he believes could be a hangar for spacecraft, as there were several of them there, each similar to the one he had seen from the truck. The man guided Walton to a room in which there were two more men and a woman; although facially different in appearance, each had the same color hair and the same perfect, blemishless, golden skin. The woman was buxom, conventionally beautiful and shapely, with shoulder-length hair. They wore no helmets and did not answer Walton when he spoke to them. Instead, they coaxed him on to a table and placed a soft oxygen mask over his mouth and nose. There were no tubes attached to the mask, only what resembled a black golfball. He quickly slipped back into unconsciousness.

Walton's next recollection is of finding himself wandering and almost hysterical on a road west of Heber. The first part of his story, the encounter in the forest, has been corroborated by the other six men, each having undergone extensive questioning. Walton also agreed to a polygraph test, which he passed. Most of the details of his 126-hour disappearance are still a mystery, but he is convinced he was not among earthlings or anything known to our scientists on earth. The six coworkers form the largest group of abduction witnesses of any publicized case. Their presence, in such a high number, even deters many skeptics from judging and discussing this case.

## Lydia Stalnaker

Twenty-five years ago, before Florida became an attraction for Northern industy and Northern families seeking to settle in the sunbelt, the area around Jacksonville was rural, filled with farms and small towns that have since been incorporated into the city limits.

One afternoon, nine-year-old Lydia Stalnaker was walking on a dirt road from a friend's house toward her parents' farm on the outskirts of Jacksonville. It was late afternoon, as she recalls now, and she was accompanied by her sister and her brother. It had been a pleasant afternoon; they had been playing, talking, and munching sweets. The trek back to the farm wasn't necessarily a long one, but the three youngsters were feeling playful, and they stopped every so often to 'fool around,' hoping to make the enjoyment of the afternoon last just a little longer.

Suddenly, they saw a bright flash, and there was a man on the road with them. The next thing the children remembered, they were running back on to the road from the thick foliage surrounding them, screaming for help and hysterically crying. The warm sun had disappeared, and it was dark. The neighbors they had been visiting came running down the road, and their parents also appeared, both parties afraid they had gotten into some trouble or stumbled upon a snake and needed help.

'We couldn't explain where we had been,' Stalnaker remembers. 'We were totally hysterical. We screamed and hollered for days, couldn't sleep. We kept saying, "They're gonna get us." My parents would ask, "Who? There's nobody in the woods." Finally, my brother blurted out that the man was a "Negro." That didn't make any sense, because there were no blacks in our part of Jacksonville. They had their own quarters in those days. And besides, they worked on the farm and we were children – we weren't afraid of them.'

For several days, the two families searched the woods for the mysterious man or some clue to what had happened but with no success. The children continued to have what Stalnaker describes as 'fearful dreams,' but they finally leveled off. She was the most affected, but in time she, too, put the unnerving experience behind her.

About nineteen years later, in August 1974, Stalnaker, then a divorcee with two daughters, was driving north from Jacksonville when she saw a bright light coming out of the sky. It was a warm August night and she pulled into a parking area off the road and got out of her car to give the bright light a second look. Another car pulled into the area, also, and the man in the car, whom Stalnaker thought she vaguely knew, joined her by the side of the road. They stared at the light hovering over some distant trees, assuming it was a helicopter, and gasped as they noticed it had descended, as if crashing, behind the trees. Fearing that there might be injured passengers, they decided to drive toward the uninhabited region to see if they could be of help.

'I asked the man if he had seen what I had seen,' she recalls. 'He said, "Yes, and it's right on time." The man was short, less than five feet five inches, and had a dark, Italian or Jewish look. I looked at my watch and it was 9 P.M. He coaxed me into his car, and we drove off to find the spot.'

As she got closer to the cluster of trees in which she assumed the crash had taken place, Stalnaker felt an uncomfortable sensation of being suffocated, as if all the air had been sucked out of the automobile. The light from the object became visible to her, but all she could think about was trying to get a good breath; she was being smothered. Her hair 'stood up on ends, but I wasn't cold.' The man driving the car asked her if she was cold, and she answered, 'No.'

'Then it seemed like just a moment passed and we were heading back towards Jacksonville on another road,' she continues. 'He was saying to me, "What happened, what happened?" but I didn't answer. My forehead was hurting, my stomach got nauseated. It was midnight, but that didn't seem possible, because it was just nine o'clock. I had no idea where we had been and suddenly I had no interest in the bright light we had gone to investigate.'

For several days, the ill feeling remained, then disappeared after, in desperation, Stalnaker had asked God to let her die or let her get well, one or the other. When the nausea and headaches faded, she felt 'fine again for several more days,' she said; then 'I kept hearing someone talk to me, telling me things.'

Although she considers herself a 'lazy type,' Stalnaker followed the instructions of these voices, which apparently wanted her to become physically fit. She consumed many different vitamins and found herself drawn to a gym for karate lessons. At the same time, she was having frightening dreams of being on an operating table surrounded by people wearing masks, who were shining bright lights in her face and sticking painful needles in her sides. The dreams would usually occur at 3:00 A.M., and when she awoke, she would find herself in odd positions, as if she had been moved.

Frightened by these nocturnal activities, Stalnaker reviewed her situation with her family. They agreed that she needed therapy of some kind, so she contacted the local mental health clinic and told them her story. They couldn't find anything physically wrong with her, but the dreams persisted, so they placed her in a group therapy session with women who had rape fantasies and dreams about men chasing them with knives. It didn't take long for Stalnaker to realize that she did not belong there.

'I had to go back to the incident, I had to find out what had really happened,' she says, her fright still evident years later. 'This was in May 1975, months after the incident, but they got me in touch with Dr. Art Winkler, a hypnotist from Arizona who happened to be in the area. I had taken to fasting and had found religion again. I needed help from somewhere; I was willing to see this doctor.'

Stalnaker discussed what had happened with Dr. Winkler, and he suggested that perhaps she had seen a UFO, a contention she refused to believe. Under hypnosis, she revealed her story, a painful tale told through a symphony of yells, screams, howls, and gasping for air so intense that the doctor snapped her out of the trance. He knew she had seen a UFO, but that was all he could say.

Adding to the mystery were two odd occurrences. While she was under hypnosis, a holly tree near the house broke in half and rolled up a hill toward the edifice. There was no wind that day, and no other holly tree was disturbed. Second, the strange-looking man who had driven her to the site had disappeared. Upon investigation, Lydia discovered that he had quit his job, but no one knew where he was. His employer said that the man had appeared in town one morning looking for work, but they did not know where he had come from. She now speculates that he was sent by the aliens to lure her to the craft.

Dr. James Harder, the APRO researcher, traveled to Jacksonville to aid Stalnaker. Through further hypnosis and a partial return of memory, she recalled being taken aboard a UFO and placed on an operating table, where she was confronted with a 'large, fearsome-looking creature with no hair, large ears sticking out from the head, small facial features – small cheek bones and mouth – but large fire-red eyes and ash gray skin.'

Also aboard the craft, she said, were two other types of aliens, who seemed to be subservient to the several large ones, but only one of the senior type spoke to her. The secondary beings included one that was robotlike, perhaps a servant of some kind. The third alien group was almost identical in looks with human beings, but with golden-tan skin and very attractive. She is not sure what that type did aboard the craft, but they were very kind and helpful.

The aliens placed her on the operating table and stuck needles or probes in her side. They tried to reassure her but were oblivious to her pain. They said she had been 'chosen for her task because of her chemistry.'

Through hypnosis, Stalnaker also recalled what had transpired when she was nine years old. At that time, she was taken aboard a craft by similar beings, who placed a clamp on her head and 'took knowledge out of my head – they knew all about me,' she says. Stalnaker was told that they would return, that she had been 'chosen.' She remembers seeing her brother and sister put through the same test but does not remember if they were given a similar explanation of the examination.

Her brother died in a car accident in 1965. Her sister has refused hypnosis, afraid that she'll have to go through 'what Lydia's been through.'

Stalnaker does not recall the specifics of the type of craft, but she says she was told the aliens were 'from a galaxy to the right of our galaxy.' She says they also have a base underneath the ocean off the coast of Florida.

## Charles Hickson and Calvin Parker

Charles Hickson, a man in his early forties, and Calvin Parker, nineteen years old, were quietly fishing at the mouth of the Pascagoula River in Mississippi on the evening of October 11, 1973. Within yards of the spot at which they decided to try their luck was the shipyard where they were employed. Hickson and the much younger Parker had met several months before when Calvin had come to nearby Gautier to work and rented a room from Hickson and his wife, Blanche.

The two men were talking and relaxing when they heard a buzzing sound of some kind. Turning to look for the source of the odd noise, they were awe stricken by what was only a few feet from them: a large egg-shaped object hovering above the ground. The craft was ten feet by eight feet and emitted the buzzing sound as if it were a pressure hose.

As the men stood motionless, a door opened in the craft and

three occupants came toward them. These aliens 'floated,' according to Hickson, and their legs did not seem to move. They were humanlike, perhaps five feet tall, with heads shaped like a bullet, no neck, a slit for a mouth, and pointed conical appendages where their noses and ears should be. No eyes were visible to Hickson and Parker. The aliens' skin color was light gray, similar to the color of an elephant, with many wrinkles. They had round feet and hands that looked like the claws of a crab.

Two of the occupants grabbed Hickson, and one took hold of Parker's arms, although by this time he had fainted. Hickson recalls that the aliens lifted him underneath his arms and floated him into the spacecraft. He is not sure what happened to Parker.

Later, under hypnosis, Hickson recalled the full details of the experience. Inside the craft was a brightly lit room without any evident source of light – no fixtures, candles, chemicals. Floating him in midair, the aliens placed an object that resembled a human eye before him. They shifted him into different positions in front of the object as if it were for examination purposes, and the object also moved on its own accord over his body.

While the examination was in progess, Hickson was able to make some mental notes on the aliens themselves. They seemed to communicate with humming sounds, and their mouth slits did not move, probably because they were unable to use them.

When the 'eye' had finished its chore, Hickson was left suspended in midair, unable to move anything but his eyes. After a few more minutes – he estimates twenty – he was floated outside the craft, where he fell over from exhaustion, feeling extremely weak. Parker was next to him, on his knees, crying and praying with hysterical fervor. Hickson watched as the craft flew straight up in the sky, making a hissing sound, and disappeared almost instantly.

Afraid of ridicule, they decided, at first, not to tell anyone of their experience but within hours had changed their minds and contacted the local air force base. They were told to call the sheriff's office, which they did. Within twenty-four hours, the news wire services had spread their story around the world.

Hickson and Parker have been forced to undergo lie detector tests and other scrutinizing methods to prove their story was no hoax. They passed all tests, at least as far as the sheriff and most researchers were concerned. At one point, they were placed in a room with hidden microphones to see if they would reveal the same stories or a hoax when placed alone. The sheriff was once again satisfied that their story was truthful since they said nothing contradictory in the bugged room. Researchers Dr. James Harder and Dr. J. Allen Hynek, who heads the Center for UFO Studies in Evanston, Illinois, were satisfied with Hickson's hypnotic recollections. It was decided that Parker was too traumatized to undergo hypnosis.

## Ellecia Gruen

A homemaker living in Ogden Center, Michigan, just outside of Blissfield, Ellecia Gruen has had several encounters rather than abductions, but the resultant changes in her life make her case one of the more exciting for several of the researchers who regularly investigate reported UFO sightings and abductions.

One day, while cleaning her house in the 'early seventies' – she can no longer pinpoint the exact day and time – Gruen found that she could not shake a very odd memory that had come into her head. In her mind's eye, she remembered when she was seven years old, living in the orphanage in which she was raised, outside of Toledo, Ohio. In the 'vision' she was in her bed in the ward of the orphanage, and there were alien creatures standing around her, running machines of some sort over her body. She remembers they were grayish in color, and their hands did not have fingers, rather 'two claws and a thumb,' the claws being similar to those of common crustaceans.

The memory came to her in stages as she was cleaning, dusting, and mopping the floors. She does not recall being unnerved by the recollections, but she was naturally puzzled. She shared the story with her husband, who was convinced it was a dream, and with friends, who offered their opinions about the possibilities of extraterrestrial life and then changed the subject.

Gruen put the events of the day behind her and went about her normal activities. She likes to bake, strip furniture, crochet, paint, and play the piano. She also had two young sons to take care of. She considered her life a rich and full one.

Then, for three months in the spring of 1976, her life was more seriously disrupted. For those three months, she was harassed by dozens of UFOs flying above and around her house. The two family German shepherds became petrified and would not leave the house. The Gruens witnessed poltergeists in their home – specifically, the appliances turned on and off without human aid.

Gruen believes there were several types of craft, some of which landed. The aliens, whom she did not see at close range, got out of the craft many times and walked around her property, leaving occasional footprints that vanished with the melting snow.

Her neighbors also witnessed the craft, which she believes came from the stars known as Pleiades in the constellation Taurus the bull. They came as close as ten feet above the driveway, and she took photographs of them.

Finally, in an exasperated move, she went outside and threatened the intruders one night. She screamed at them to 'get out of my sky space.'

'I yelled and yelled,' she recalls. 'It looked as if the big dipper dissolved and came towards me, but I held my ground. I said I wasn't afraid of them and if they wanted to do something to me, to do it and get it over with.'

'The stars in the big dipper seemed to change to spacecrafts flying over a field,' she continues. 'That's hard to believe, but that's the truth.'

The last sighting, made by a neighbor, was of a large red craft hovering over the Gruen home soon after Mrs. Gruen's confrontation.' There have been no sightings since.

Gruen has never been hypnotized, nor has she ever taken a

lie detector test, as have so many other abductees. However, she has been in close touch with researchers, parapsychologists, and other interested parties.

A mysterious but substantiated addition to the files some researchers have on Ellecia Gruen is the story of a woman who, because she will not go public, will be referred to as 'Mrs. K.' Her story, however mind boggling it may appear to some, is identical to Gruen's. She was in the same orphanage ward and had the same recollection of aliens running machines over her body. Later, through a coincidence both find peculiar, Gruen and Mrs. K. found themselves living in tiny Ogden Center, primarily a residential community. Both were harassed by the same group of UFOs. Mrs. K. is a deeply religious woman who is convinced that the spacecraft were sent by a satanic force. She has become more devout in prayer and refuses to believe that alien creatures might come from distant planets. Because of this fundamentalism, she will not cooperate with researchers, and her story is incomplete in detail.

## Jeffrey Greenhaw

A graduate of the Alabama State Police Academy, Jeffrey Greenhaw was barely twenty-three years old when he was elected police chief of rural Falkville, a community with a population of twelve hundred not far from his parents' home in Hartselle. Well liked in the area, Greenhaw was considered a model police officer, never derelict in duty and often praised by his superiors at the Morgan County sheriff's office.

On the evening of October 17, 1973, Greenhaw had heard a report from a woman in Falkville of a UFO in the vicinity. The woman, whose name has never been disclosed, claimed that she had seen a spacecraft land. Although skeptical about UFOs, Greenhaw said he would keep an eye out for anything suspicious while driving in his car on his normal patrol routes.

Between 10:30 and 11:00 P.M., Greenhaw spotted an odd figure standing in the middle of a road west of Falkville. He stopped the car and was amazed at what he saw. The creature was five foot six inches tall, well-proportioned, humanlike with a lanky frame. It wore a shiny one-piece space suit that was covered with what Greenhaw described as 'tinfoil material.' Its legs were covered with tight, thigh-length boots, and it wore mittens on its hands and a pointed helmet. No facial features were visible from underneath a protective visor. Its walk was stiff, and there were no audible sounds.

Greenhaw reached into the back of his patrol car and pulled out a Polaroid camera he routinely carried for police reports: mug shots, photographs of burglaries, and the like. In the course of a few minutes, he took four clear photos of the creature, one from fifty feet away, one as the creature moved to about twenty feet away, and two more as the creature came as close as ten feet away from Greenhaw.

Unexpectedly. as Greenhaw flashed a blue light from the car console in its direction, the creature turned and began to bound down the road.

'He didn't run like we would,' Greenhaw remembers. 'He was running from side to side, and it looked like he had springs under his feet to propel him. He could go ten feet in one step. I got into the car, but in my excitement, I stepped down too hard on the accelerator and the car skidded almost into a ditch. By the time I got back on the road the alien was gone. I looked for him in the pastures, but could see nothing.'

About half an hour after the encounter, Greenhaw dropped by the local newspaper office to tell the local editor about what had happened. The pictures and his story were distributed by worldwide news agencies.

During the next few days, he was contacted by several government officials who said that there had been other sightings and reports of aliens seen on the ground. In fact, the air force admitted that it had tracked an unidentified bleep on radar but had lost it near Falkville. However, the government and the military refused to release their findings. Greenhaw was the only person willing to tell the public. He says he regarded it as a matter of duty.

## DIRECT ENCOUNTERS

### JESSICA ROLFE

Jessica Rolfe is the pseudonym we use for an actress-writer living in Los Angeles. She is a secret abductee who believes it is best if her true identity remains unknown.

Now twenty-seven years old, Jessica's encounters began when she was five years old, living with her adoptive parents and older sister in Miami Beach, Florida. One night, soon after she had been tucked into bed, her windows wide open, she said that three 'men' appeared, materializing out of thin air. Jessica describes them as tall, with gold-colored, blemishless skin, gold-brown hair, well-proportioned frames, and mouths that did not move when they communicated. They looked remarkably like human beings. One of the men came to her side, lifted her from bed, and asked telepathically, 'Would you like to come with us now?' There was a pause as he gestured out the window, and Jessica replied, 'No, I like it here.' The man told her that was all right, he tucked her back into bed, and they disappeared. Jessica jumped up, threw off the covers, ran into her parents' room, and asked them who the men were. They told her she had been dreaming.

Between the ages of five and fourteen, she said, different alien men of the same race returned often to her bedside. It became almost a ritual. They would sit with her, giving her lessons in their ways and in their version of the history of creation. When she was fourteen, Jessica was allowed, rather 'chose,' to ride in their craft, which she says are 'more simple' than we would expect. 'They are powered by a combination of magnetic energy and the energy of the navigator,' she says. 'They are incredibly strong. One fifty-foot ship could tow Earth from its orbit and they can travel right through the sun.'

Through the years, Rolfe coined the name *Kuran* for the alien race. After the death of her adoptive father in 1977, Rolfe finally confided her experiences to her mother. Much to the contactee's surprise, her mother took it quite calmly. She admitted, in fact, that she had suspected something for quite some time. Her mother related that she had often heard Jessica speaking out loud in her room at night as if holding a conversation and that on other occasions she would open the door to the room late at night and find the girl gone. Yet, because of some inner feeling, the mother never became worried or frightened during Jessica's absence.

Her mother also remembered that Rolfe's father had suspected that there was something unusual about his daughter. As a teenager, Jessica was allowed to move into the converted garage that was attached to the house. Her father would put the family cat out each night and would find it odd that often the cat would be either back in the kitchen or in Jessica's room in the morning, though no family member had let her in.

According to Rolfe, the *Kuran* communicate telepathically, but they do have vocal sounds for emotional responses such as 'look there,' 'watch out,' 'wow,' or expressions of that nature in their own language. She believes that this race lives in several bases on earth, including some off the coasts of Florida and Argentina and one in the Amazon basin. They have lived on Earth apart from humans for millions of years, she feels, although they have made themselves known to us from time to time. Living in a culture in which imagination is paramount and murder, hatred, boundaries, and ethnic polarization are unknown, they find it as difficult to fathom humans as we would find it difficult to understand their ways.

Rolfe contends that the *Kuran* have confided much of their knowledge in her. They are 'militaristic' but not in a warlike sense. Rather, in our galaxy, they are an extremely high form of evolution and often absorb other races into their own. As far as Earth is concerned, they are guides and protectors, often accompanying other alien races on their tours here. Rolfe has been told of twelve alien races that have visited Earth.

The version of creation and human existence on Earth that Rolfe believes has been revealed to her differs greatly from the conventional Biblical account of Genesis.

As Rolfe tells it, in the beginning, our race lived on a planet that broke into many pieces and now is seen as the asteroid belt between Mars and Jupiter. Before the destruction of this

## DIRECT ENCOUNTERS

planet by natural forces, the *Kuran* visited its inhabitants and offered to bring them to another suitable place if they would live by the *Kuran* laws, unspecified to Rolfe. Even though the humans had no means of escaping their planet, they rejected the offer. Two groups did manage to escape. One ended up on a planet in the constellation known as Pegasus. The other group, our ancestors, somehow ended up on Earth. Earth was a planet the *Kuran* had wanted these beings to avoid.

It seems that Earth had not sufficiently evolved to accept a highly advanced and harmonic people; harmonic is the word Jessica uses to describe a race that is at peace with itself and understands the concept of oneness of people and energy. On Earth, there was a multitude of species – insects, reptiles, mammals, plants that ate insects, animals that ate other animals – and an unpredictable weather system. All in all, not a spot conducive to the life style the humans had known. Earth was a tough place on which to live.

However, even then humans were an arrogant people. Our ancestors, whom Rolfe says we know under the label 'Cro-Magnon,' conquered the earth. They forced the birds into the sky. Neanderthal and other prehistoric humanoids ceased to exist. The creatures who were then the developing race on Earth were forced to live in the sea, where we now call them dolphins. Even today, the dolphins use the telepathic, emotional, and sound form of communication typical of higher beings. According to the history told to Jessica, they are actual native intelligent life on earth.

Retaining the claim to the land was also not easy for the immigrant humans. Other alien races wanted to dock here, but they were forced away. One of these groups, unable to leave for lack of vehicles, took to the colder regions and the remote corners of the planet. Their remaining souls are frequently seen and have been given the name Big Foot or Sasquatch.

Earth in those days consisted of one huge land mass surrounded by water, the land mass called 'Mu' by the humans. As the first immigrant generations of Mu died out, and new sons and daughters were born, the memory of the migration became less clear. The storehouse of original knowledge was zealously guarded by the leaders, called magi*. The magi were an unscrupulous lot, as each wanted to rule. So each magi took his followers to a different section of Mu, and boundaries were established to protect ownership and arable lands.

This move led to the development of different verbal languages as well as nations that were in competition and conflict with each other. The magi were well aware that there was only a finite number of souls, each capable of returning in another form after death, the population, however, always remaining constant, not growing but recycling itself. More people were needed to compete with other magis, so they began tampering with the earth's energy sources and harnessed enough atomic matter to create 'mutant souls.'

These souls knew nothing of the past; their attitudes were different, and they were sometimes caught in energy warps when they died; thus, instead of recycling, they became ghosts, which Rolfe describes as the form we take when the soul has left the body but a perception of the form remains. Again, this was unheard of in all the galaxy.

The *Kuran*, who had witnessed this misuse of energy, returned to Earth to offer the humans a chance to get back on the right track. Many of the original souls agreed to follow the *Kuran*, but the magi and the mutant souls balked. The *Kuran* and their followers built what we now call the mythical Atlantis, a harmonic paradise. The jealousy of the residents of Mu got the better of them, and they set out to destroy Atlantis. The *Kuran* dismantled the paradise, hiding it from the earthlings, but the Muites set off the atomic explosion, anyway, causing the Earth to reverse the spin of its axis. This, in turn, wreaked havoc on the environment, and the ice caps grew and slithered down the earth, resulting in an Ice Age, tearing

---

*Magi: In common usage, the priestly caste in ancient Medea and Persia, supposedly having occult powers. In the Bible, the word appears as the wise men from the East bringing gifts to Jesus.

apart the land mass and creating the continents we know today. Survival became even more acute for the earthlings, and by the time the ice retreated, most of those who had survived had virtually no knowledge of the migration and the powers they once had. Some magi remained.

From time to time, Rolfe says she was told, the *Kuran* have made themselves known to the earthlings, sometimes over the rage of the magi, but the contact has never worked out. The humans, now decidedly primitive, would look to the *Kuran* for leadership, but the *Kuran* did not want to lead in our terms. Accidentally, they have found themselves pharaohs of Egypt, gods on Olympus, and communicating through radio crystals in the Holy Ark of the Covenant.

'As I understand it, every time they have tried to be with us, they have botched it,' says Rolfe, a woman short in stature with blondish hair and a mature, intense look. 'I may have been chosen because my soul may be an original one. Other races have also made themselves known to humans, particularly a grayish-white people who lived underground and were mistakenly revered as Druids.'

Rolfe adds that the *Kuran* have no concept of God or religion but do believe there is a creator of the universe. This creator does not become involved in the day to day activities of our lives. Rolfe likens their philosophy to that of Benedict Spinoza, the Dutch philosopher, and the pantheistic view that there is no transcendent God and that God is the whole of the universe.

This collection of information makes it rather clear why Rolfe has chosen to confide in only a few close friends and is wary of going public.

However far-fetched or bizarre her story may seem, she insists that even in earthly books there are theories and conjectures to support the history of creation she tells. Atlantis and Mu are places that have passed down from ancient myths and legends. Plato tells us that the ancient Egyptians believed in the existence of Atlantis, a place that by Egyptian calculations existed twelve thousand years ago. Rolfe explains that geologists and anthropologists do feel that the continents were once together and were split by either the natural movements of the Earth or some cataclysmic activity. She maintains that we are not really descended from many of the prehistoric human apelike beings, that the line of Zinjanthropus is a dead end, and it is reasonable, Rolfe asserts, to assume that dolphins were land mammals that returned to the sea. Some scientists have speculated that the Earth's axis has changed and that there could have been a natural atomic explosion of some kind many years ago, perhaps causing the formation of the moon.

Rolfe admits to extensive reading in these areas, and she says she can direct skeptics to books that will back up many of her statements, and, indeed, those books exist.

An interesting sidenote to her story occurred as she was standing in a field in New Hampshire during a vacation and spotted a UFO one night. She made telepathic communication with the aliens on the spacecraft, and, she says, when she returned home, they visited her. The aliens said they were attracted by the yellow jumpsuit she had been wearing and that they came from Reticuli, the same star system as the Hills' captors. The aliens were grayish in color, five feet tall, with slits for mouths, five fingers to each hand, and large slanted eyes, according to Rolfe.

Even the most seasoned UFO investigators admit that it is difficult to ascertain patterns or common ground in the nature of the abductions. The abductees can be grouped by some of the information they have about alien races, the nature of their abductions, and in the descriptions they have given of the beings themselves, but there is not one category in which one can fit every abduction.

For example, Jessica Rolfe's description of the *Kuran* – golden colored, blemishless skin, tall, well proportioned – matches the description of the human-looking aliens whom Travis Walton and Lydia Stalnaker encountered and could be similar to Carl Higdon's 'high-yellow' beings since color can vary according to individual perception and available light.

In addition, Higdon, Stalnaker, and Rolfe all speak of the aliens having a base off the coast of Florida.

Betty Hill, Travis Walton, Louise Smith, Mona Stafford, and Jessica Rolfe have seen white or gray aliens, four to five feet tall, with slits for mouths and either human hands or lobsterlike claws and fingers. Again, there are similarities in the large, slightly slanted eyes, although the costumes the beings wore were different in each case. One unexplainable coincidence is that both Jessica Rolfe and Betty Hill have determined the aliens from this group are from Reticuli. Both describe the aliens the same way, and both speak of the aliens' fascination with the color yellow. Since Rolfe has not read the book on the Hill experience, nor was it determined until 1972 that Betty Hill's abduction was by visitors from Reticuli, it seems unlikely to believers that the two women concocted this seemingly minor bit of information. While not conclusive by any means, it adds credence to their statements.

Another coincidence is that while Rolfe speaks of her *Kuran* as guides and protectors, Walton mentions aliens of similar description who delivered him from the other race on the craft. Stalnaker also speaks of the 'tan or golden type' as serving a helpful purpose.

Looking at the abductions again, there is an imperfect pattern. While most of the captures took place in open areas, often as the humans were driving down a quiet highway or road, the aliens in Ellecia Gruen's case were brazen enough to fly right over Ogden Center for a three-month period where, she says, they were observed by hundreds of people and, adding to the confusion in patterns, originally examined her at her bedside in an orphanage. Rolfe, too, was contacted in her own home, as was Mona Stafford during her second encounter.

If there is a common denominator, it does not seem to be directly related to the aliens *unless* they have much more control over who their victims will be than we can imagine. The people abducted outside their homes were in a place they normally would not have been or had not previously planned to be or were drawn by impulse to venture into an unknown area.

This fact, that the abductees were somewhere they did not intend to be, does tie many of the cases together. Carl Higdon went hunting in a zone few ever dared wander into; Lydia Stalnaker was mysteriously drawn into an isolated forest outside Jacksonville; Travis Walton was on a bumpy road and felt compelled to leap from the truck to investigate the craft while his friends sat dumbfounded; Louise Smith, Mona Stafford, and Elaine Thomas had not planned to drive to Stanford for dinner; it was a spontaneous decision. In fact, Stafford was due at her sister's house for dinner that night. Betty and Barney Hill had taken a spur-of-the-moment vacation, so poorly planned that they did not even have enough cash for a motel room on that fateful night. Charles Hickson and Calvin Parker did not often fish at that spot.

Human beings, especially Americans, have an inbred need to feel they are in control of their lives and have freedom of choice, so it is not surprising that most of the abductees dismiss any notion that the aliens had planned to pick them up, that their selection was anything but a random one. Higdon insists the aliens told him he 'was not what they were looking for.' The Hills, the women from Kentucky, Hickson and Parker, all feel their selection came without advance planning. Mona Stafford now speculates that her day was unusual from the moment she got up but also admits that she may be searching for a reason.

The second visit by aliens to Gruen and Stalnaker and perhaps every visit to Rolfe could be construed as preordained. Stalnaker claims she was told she was chosen 'because of my chemistry.' Rolfe's tie with her *Kuran* is a highly developed relationship, but even she admits that associations with strange beings have come by accident.

Finding a conclusive purpose for the abductions is even more challenging. 'On us it was more a physical examination,' ponders Betty Hill, who has herself become a UFO investigator. 'On Hickson and Parker, there was no physical, they just sort of circled their bodies with some sort of light, took 'em back and took off. As for the three women from Kentucky, apparently they were interested there in seeing how much pain they could tolerate. It seems to me we are each a different facet of their experiment, or investigation of people on Earth,' says Betty Hill.

Whatever the scenario of each account, the reality of being seized by a UFO was not something easily grasped by these abductees. Many of them wanted to believe it was a psychotic delusion – for that can be cured – or a dream or a hypnogogic state.

None of these alternatives seems to fit. They knew they were sane. No psychologist, psychiatrist, or other professional would treat them for a delusion. Not one abductee had a history of mental illness or a messiah complex.

What bothered them most was not fears of ill health but a lack of knowledgeable individuals to whom they could turn. Books they could read often revealed bizarre tales of hoaxes and charlatans. The abductees were also searching for patterns, something that would unite them with each other. What they found was what perhaps annoys the skeptics most. There is no abductee stereotype, no way to label them or fit them neatly into a statistical pattern. These people are individuals no matter how different their stories may be.

They are all alike in one overriding way. Each has to cope with the fact that he has had an experience that challenges the limits of human knowledge. Each must live his daily life in the shadows of this discovery, particularly if he has 'gone public.' Their lives can never again be described as 'typical.' Their perceptions of themselves and their communities and the world's conception of them have taken on new dimensions.

Chapter Two

# What the Record Shows

UFO abductees face two major problems when they become convinced that they did, indeed, encounter alien beings.

First, they have no tangible evidence to substantiate their claims. Therefore, there are many nonbelievers, often from the most respected levels of science and the media. On occasion, there is evidence acceptable to the abductee such as the photographs taken by Ellecia Gruen or Jeffrey Greenhaw, but no photograph by itself can eliminate all doubt.

Second, many of the abductees – Travis Walton, Betty Hill, and Mona Stafford, for example – say that they themselves were reluctant to believe what happened at first because they had never heard of such a thing happening to anyone else. Only recently have lists of encounters and UFO sightings begun to attract so much attention. It still takes a great deal of research to uncover other encounters.

Generally, the abductee has little to say to those who argue that an abduction is implausible. Charges that the witness, if not deluded, could be suffering from a post-World War II syndrome caused by overexposure to modern aerospace achievements are usually ignored. Skeptics attribute abductee claims to 'Buck Rogers' hallucinations about spacemen triggered by the overwhelming growth of sophisticated technology.

In fact, however, UFOs are a worldwide phenomenon.

## WHAT THE RECORD SHOWS

There have been sightings on every continent, in areas of sophisticated technology and areas that can only be described as backward. Similar types of UFOs and encounters have been described by witnesses, often with no knowledge of the experiences of others.

Some theorists hold to the belief that extraterrestrials have been visiting earthlings since the beginning of recorded history. Theories, many embraced by UFO scholars, abound about the extraterrestrial implications in the Bible (see Chapter Eight), but on a more secular level, many authors have speculated about unusual writings and carvings created by ancient civilizations.

Some of the more conceivable of these ancient writings, in the estimation of UFO believers, are the Sumero-Babylonian accounts of fiery-looking eggs landing with beings inside; the Mayan stone carvings of what might be interpreted as a being in a space suit; and the writings of the Judean historian Josephus, who saw an object in the sky over Jerusalem, of which he wrote: 'There was a star resembling a sword which stood over the city and a comet that continued a whole year' (Josephus in *War of the Jews*, Book Six).

Of course, for the abductees looking for shreds of evidence to show the world, conjecture about ancient peoples will not suffice. There is no way to compose a definite interpretation.

Moving through the archives to modern times, when literacy and record keeping without embellishments can be expected, the abductee will discover that the appearance of unknown sky vehicles in the latter half of the nineteenth century was not entirely uncommon. In the years when airplanes were still a dream and even manned balloons a rarity, objects were seen in the heavens throughout the United States and Western Europe. According to Gardner Soule in *UFOs and IFOs; a Factual Report on Flying Saucers*, in 1871, for example, a large round object hovered over Marseilles, France, for fifteen minutes and was viewed by hundreds of people. Similarly, in 1875, a cigar-shaped flying object terrified the residents of Bonham, Texas, one afternoon; in March 1880, brilliantly glowing objects were seen by residents of Kattenau, Germany, in the sky above their town.

Thousands of miles away, in California, reported Soule, a somewhat better known series of encounters and sightings known as the 'California Airship Flap' began brewing in 1896, still several years before the Wright brothers' historic flight. During a two-year period, hundreds of Californians from all parts of the state reported seeing brightly lighted craft in the sky and heard the sounds of human voices, frequently singing or humming, in the vehicles.

While the Californians were seeing flying vehicles – no doubt the first flying vehicles of any kind they had seen – an incident in Aurora, Texas, on April 19, 1897, continues to have repercussions today.

According to *The New York Times*, a Dallas newspaper story of the period reported that a cigar-shaped airship, which had been seen in many parts of the state, crashed into Judge J. S. Proctor's home on that fateful spring day.

An unusually small 'man' – as recorded then – similar in description to the aliens seen by the Hills, Travis Walton, and Jessica Rolfe and believed to be the pilot of the vehicle, fell out of the craft during the crash and was dead by the time Judge Proctor reached him. The other occupants of the airship took off in the craft immediately, making no effort to rescue their comrade. The residents of Aurora are alleged to have buried the little man in the local cemetery.

Recently, UFO students have repeatedly attempted to exhume the remains of the humanoid but have been prevented from doing so by the Aurora Cemetery Association and the residents themselves because no one seems to remember which grave belongs to the unknown pilot and they do not wish to have the entire grounds overturned. The humanoid's grave marker disappeared mysteriously a number of years ago, no doubt neglected for most of the century.

Recorded sightings, particularly in Great Britain and France, continued with some regularity until World War I when the increased use of airplanes made the novelty of vehicles in the sky less acute. Yet events from the previous century seem distant, intangible, like the alleged sightings of the Mayans or Judeans. The UFO witnesses of today seem to gain comfort from knowing that their contemporaries had the same experiences.

The abductees are reassured to learn of thousands of UFO sightings since World War II, many documented in newspapers and popular books published during the last three decades in all parts of the globe.

Increased interest in the possibility of extraterrestrial life began more than a decade before human technology was able to launch a spacecraft into the outer atmosphere. On June 24, 1947, Kenneth Arnold, a businessman, was piloting his private airplane near Mount Rainier, Washington. Mr. Arnold spotted nine disclike vehicles flying to the north of the peak. He described the in-flight motion of these discs as looking like 'a saucer skipping across the water,' thus coining the term 'flying saucer.'

One month after the hoopla caused by Arnold's sighting and the resultant phenomena, christened with the new phrase 'flying saucer,' came the first report of an actual sighting of UFO occupants. Actually, this close encounter was not in the United States but far south in Brazil, which, like other South American countries, began a decade earlier recording frequent UFO sightings, usually by working people who had no knowledge of the discovery near Mount Rainier.

According to Gordon Creighton in 'The Humanoids in Latin America,' reported in *The Humanoids* (Charles Bowen, editor), the July 1947 encounter in Brazil involved a road-working crew who heard a piercing whistle and then saw a huge silver disc, roughly 150 feet in diameter, land in a nearby field. All but one of the men fled, as in the Travis Walton incident many years later. In contrast to the Walton incident, the disc did not send out a light beam to stun the Brazilian who remained. Rather, the vehicle landed, and three seven-foot-tall beings in transparent suits emerged.

The visitors approached the worker but did not attack him.

According to the man, they attempted to communicate by drawing a map or chart on the ground. He ran away and hid in brush not far from the road, but he could see them from his vantage point cavorting about for almost an hour, acting in a manner similar to the way American astronauts first behaved when testing the gravity on the moon. Then the three aliens reentered the craft and took off as abruptly as they had landed.

Three years later, reported Creighton, in Argentina, a rancher watched an identical spacecraft and its tall, transparently attired occupants, who stepped out on to his grazing land. When the aliens spotted him, they hurried back toward their craft, and the rancher dashed toward his house. The description of this meeting, in the Argentinian's words, sounded like an unplanned scene from a silent slapstick movie.

As interest grew worldwide, news items about UFO sightings and encounters were circulated by all the major news services – Associated Press, United Press, International News Service, and Reuters – with articles appearing on the back pages of major newspapers and somewhat more prominently in the weekly tabloids.

Reuters reported that on June 30, 1950, a British pilot was flying over the Atlantic Ocean at 19,000 feet when he saw a large and circular object about five miles from his own position. He radioed the U.S. Air Force base at Goose Bay, Labrador, but by the time a jet fighter reached the scene, the UFO was gone.

During the same year, several trained aircraft engineers and meteorologists in Mexico City, Mexico, admitted they could find no logical explanation for the 'four flying saucers' seen over Mexico City and Monterrey, 350 miles north. According to a United Press International report, the official observers, while not committing themselves to the UFO frenzy, did admit that there had indeed been four 'flying bodies' in the sky.

As interest increased, several nations organized research centers for the study of UFOs. One of the first was a 'flying saucer sighting station,' built in 1953 under the auspices of the

Canadian government near Shirley's Bay, ten miles southwest of Ottawa, the capital city. According to Canadian Press, the wire service, the purpose of the center was to 'prove or disprove the existence of flying saucers.' The demand for answers from a curious public was that great.

Without answers from the Canadian government or any of the private-funded UFO groups that had begun to spring up in different parts of the world, the sightings and encounters continued.

A terrifying encounter – one that could even be described as macabre – occurred in Flatwoods, in the hills of West Virginia, on September 12, 1952, and was described in *Project Blue Book*, the complete report of the U.S. Air Force UFO investigations, edited by Brad Steiger. The article said that six teenagers had seen a fiery, saucer-shaped aircraft land on a nearby hilltop. After some persuasion, the mother of two of the teens was convinced that she should climb the hill with the youths to investigate the sighting. Perhaps it had been a strange airplane and someone was hurt, they thought at the time.

What they found after the difficult climb was hardly an airplane. A large, glowing vehicle stood before them, guarded by a hideous, eight-foot tall humanoid with a blood-red face, huge green eyes, and claws for hands. The little group did not investigate any further, nor did they wait to find out if the alien was friendly. They took off down the hill as fast as they could move their legs, driven by panic and terror. The next day, the youths returned with the sheriff, only to find the area deserted but with an unpleasant sulfuric odor lingering in the air.

The Flatwoods incident has few researched counterparts, but a 1953 case in Mexico does compare with more recent encounters.

As reconstructed by Gordon Creighton in *The Humanoids*, a cab driver was underneath his automobile trying to make emergency repairs along the side of a rarely traveled road when he noticed two pairs of legs and feet standing within his partially blocked view. According to news-service reports, he came out from under the car and found himself face to face with two little men about four and a half feet tall.

One of the pair, presumably the leader, used broken Spanish to invite the cab driver to follow the aliens to their spacecraft, which also was described in almost identical terms with the Hills' vehicle seen in 1961 and the craft seen by Travis Walton in 1975; it was round, shaped like two soup bowls inverted on each other, and had large portholes and a glass dome.

The aliens tried to convince the cab driver to enter the craft, but he decided discretion was the better part of valor and ran away. The humanoids did not give chase.

France offered its own UFO controversy in 1954. While digging through the archives in the town of Arras in early 1954, a clerk found a report: 'Was seen in the sky a brilliant object somewhat like an iron bar, long and large as half the moon. It was clearly seen for fifteen minutes; then suddenly the strange object began to rise in spirals to twist and writhe like a watch spring and disappear in the sky.' The Associated Press report, circulated worldwide, ended with the startling fact that this apparent citing of a UFO was not recent; it had been written in 1461.

The Arras discovery led to a series of sightings. In October 1954, according to UFO specialist Jacques Vallée ('The Pattern Behind the UFO Landings,' in *The Humanoids*), there came a report from Britanny, where a baker said he was drawing water out of his well one night when he glanced up and saw a saucer-shaped vehicle landing ten feet to his left. Stunned, he barely moved as a door to the craft opened and a little humanoid, roughly three or four feet tall, emerged, his oval-shaped face dominated by two huge eyes. The being tried to communicate with the baker in a language other than French, and the Frenchman screamed for help. The alien quickly returned to the vehicle and was gone before help, and witnesses, could arrive.

Revelations such as these, coupled with an earlier report from October 1953 in which a woman in Haute-Marne,

France, claimed to have spoken to a strange, four-foot-tall man who muttered a few words and jumped into a spaceship and flew off into the clouds, triggered national hysteria about UFOs that lasted for more than a year.

Throughout France, reports of encounters were common. Such a trend was created that *Time* magazine did a feature on the rash of witnesses in October 1954. The aliens, who were usually identified by the contactees as 'Martians,' flew in crafts resembling flying cigars, crowns, comets, winged mushrooms, and pots and pans. One alien, who stopped a Monsieur Roger Barrault near the town of Lavoux, wore rubbers on his feet and spoke Latin. Other space travelers were seen in a variety of colors; there were blue Martians, pink Martians, and yellow ones.

Of course, not all these accounts were plausible, even to the most diehard UFO believer. The French press made light of the situation, printing cartoons and writing lampooning social columns about Martians spending romantic weekends in Vienna.

Still, despite the fun and games, thousands of people in France and in other parts of Europe were convinced they had been seeing unidentified objects in the sky. The *New York Herald Tribune* reported in December 1954 that defense agencies in Sweden, Yugoslavia, and Italy had announced they would launch a serious inquiry into the UFO sightings and pay particular attention to photographs of purported UFOs. The story added that the U.S. Air Force's Air Technical Intelligence Center, based near Dayton, Ohio, also offered to review the photographs and other information that year. In the eyes of some, UFOs had become serious business.

Not one of these investigations has advanced any definitive explanation for the phenomenon of UFOs, but from a believer's standpoint, the evidence that extraterrestrial visitation was a reality continued to mount. Newspapers in the United States began talking somewhat facetiously about 'a flying saucer season,' an unpredictable event. The expression actually referred to the fact that when there was one sighting in a particular area, others were sure to follow.

The *New York World-Telegram* gave extensive coverage to photographs taken by Warren Siegmond, a television technician, in May 1955, which depicted a spherical-shaped object moving soundlessly over the water towers of Manhattan.

On May 21, a few days after Siegmond's photographs were taken, Dorothy Kilgallen, the late syndicated columnist, wrote that she had proof that British scientists had identified the wreckage of a mysterious flying craft as having originated on another planet. According to the widely read Kilgallen, the source for this information was a 'British official of Cabinet rank,' who said: 'It's frightening, but there is no denying the flying saucers come from another planet.'

Indeed, 1955 did turn out to be 'flying saucer season' in the United States. Three months after the Siegmond photographs and the Kilgallen column were published, one of the most unusual alien encounters of the decade was recorded by local newspapers in Kentucky.

The site was halfway between the village of Kelly and the town of Hopkinsville in the southwestern corner of the state, several hundred miles from where Mona Stafford, Elaine Thomas, and Louise Smith would be abducted twenty-one years later.

*Project Blue Book* documents indicate that it was Sunday evening, August 21. The Sutton family was entertaining friends at their rural farm. Suddenly, a large, glowing flying craft landed about two hundred feet from the farmhouse. The entire group of eight adults and three children watched as five little men, less than four feet tall, with large round heads and huge yellowish eyes, approached them.

The little men stopped as they reached the edge of the light emanating from the house, seemingly sensitive to the brightness of the bulbs. The Suttons panicked and grabbed their shotguns. They kept firing at the little humanoids, watching as round after round ricocheted off the aliens' bodies. The extraterrestrials seemed to enjoy the game. For four hours, they somersaulted, rolled around, and climbed all over the fences, barn, and trees while the terrified Kentuckians tried to chase them off. At no time did the aliens return the fire or in any way threaten the frightened farmers.

More fuel was added to the growing controversy two years later when, on March 9, 1957, a Pan American Airways flight en route from New York to San Juan almost collided with what the pilot, Captain Matthew A. Van Winkle, described as 'an object with a very bright core and a fringe of green.' To avoid this UFO, which was also seen by a pilot on another aircraft, the Pan Am pilot had been forced to climb steeply to a dangerously high altitude, causing several injuries among the passengers. According to a United Press International story, Captain Van Winkle insisted during an inquiry that the object he had seen was 'definitely not a meteor.'

The first internationally reported abduction by aliens came in September 1957 when a Brazilian law professor named Joao de Freitas Guimaraes revealed that he had been sunning on the beach the summer before when a sixty-foot vehicle suddenly appeared before him. Two six-foot-tall men emerged from the disc-shaped craft, and Guimaraes tried to speak in Portuguese, English, French, and other languages but received no response.

Then the professor realized that the strange men were communicating telepathically and were inviting him aboard the spaceship. The aliens, who had blond hair, green eyes, and yellowish clothing, were very reassuring, and Guimaraes entered the craft and went on a voyage with the extraterrestrials 'somewhere outside earth's atmosphere.' In an hour, he was returned to the beach, dazed, but none the worse for wear.

The professor agreed to lecture about his experience. However, according to *Time* magazine, his first televised appearance in Brazil included a studio audience, which greeted Guimaraes with laughter and taunts, a scene with which many abductees can empathize. His pride damaged, Guimaraes retreated into his privacy, but until Barney and

Betty Hill revealed their own abduction experience in 1964, he was the most publicized abductee in the world.

During the next few years, UFOs were frequently sighted throughout Europe and South America. A Swedish army captain claimed to have seen a satellite heading toward the moon in late 1957. The Swede, who requested anonymity at the time, told the Associated Press, 'The object looked like a flattened sphere. Its sides were somewhat elongated and there was a flickering glow as from burning exhaust gas on one side.' Flying saucers were seen in the skies over Milan, Italy, and Rome, Italy, in 1958 and 1959.

On January 8 and 24, 1959, scores of people sighted an unidentified object in the sky above Balboa in the Panama Canal Zone. According to a brief article in *The New York Times*, the United States radar station at the canal tracked the object for quite some time but failed to identify it. The craft was described as 'bright silver' and traveled in a 'sweeping arc.'

Radio Australia broadcast a story that was discussed in depth by UFO experts. In September 1959, the Rev. William Gill, a missionary, said that while he was visiting a remote outpost near Boilanai in northern New Guinea, he saw a flying saucer circle at low altitude.

'With my own eyes I saw several human figures inside,' Reverend Gill told Radio Australia. 'I watched the four figures appear on top of the saucer and I have no doubt that they were human. Two of the figures seemed to be doing something near the centre of the saucer. One of the figures seemed to be standing looking down at me. I waved to the figure and to my surprise he waved back. I flashed a torch at the saucer and it apparently acknowledged by making several waving motions back and forth.'

Like the abductees in America, Gill found few believers and declined to appear in the forefront of the rising UFO debate. By the beginning of the 1960s, space travel was no longer considered mere science fiction. The Soviet Union had launched Sputnik I in 1957, and both that country and the

## WHAT THE RECORD SHOWS

United States were busily involved in a 'space race,' the goal being to land on the moon first.

Similar reports of sightings and encounters continued into the 1960s; the Hills' revelation in 1964 was the most explosive. By the middle of the decade, there were UFO investigative groups in many countries, sometimes financed by the governments.

The Soviet Union's study center, called the UFO Investigation Commission, a subcommittee of the All Union Cosnautics Commission, is probably the most active in the world. Although there has been dispute about the need for such a group, particularly among young Communist party members, the Moscow regime seems to recognize the existence of UFOs and has indicated that the planet earth may be receiving radio signals from civilizations in other solar systems.

In December 1967, Prof. Felike Zigel, the astronomer who heads the commission, called on scientists throughout the world to join together to investigate UFOs. In a statement released through Tass, the Soviet news agency, and published by *The New York Times*, Dr. Zigel said, 'Unfortunately, certain scientists both in the Soviet Union and in the United States deny the very existence of the problem [of UFOs] instead of helping to solve it.'

Six years later, in October, 1973, Prof. Samuel Kaplan of Gorky University detected strange radio impulses from all four of the radio signal receiving stations within the Soviet Union. Tass released a report that said it had been determined the 'signals could not have originated from a man-made source.'

One hundred twenty independent UFO groups exist throughout the world. All of them cannot be listed here, but a few of the more active in the past decade are: the British UFO Research Association (England), the Essex UFO Study Group (England), the Circulo de Estudios sobre Objetos No Identificados (Spain), Sociedad Brasileira de Estudos sobre Discos Voadores (Brazil), the Gaucho UFO Investigation

Group (Brazil), and the Unidentified Flying Objects Investigation Centre (Australia).

In France, UFO study is divided between two groups that have governmental blessings and support. All information about sightings is handled by the Groupement d'Études des Phénomènes Aériens. If it is decided that a particular case warrants a more comprehensive scientific examination, the information is turned over to the Centre Nationale d'Études Spatiales.

A desire to study UFOs obviously exists around the world. In a 1977 survey conducted by Prof. Peter A. Sturrok, an astronomer at Stanford University, 53 percent of the members of the American Astronomical Society said that UFOs should be investigated further, and another 27 percent said that they leaned in that direction, although they would not commit themselves to a call for UFO research just yet.

The March 1977 release of Professor Sturrok's survey was one of the catalysts of the October 1977 debate in the UN General Assembly, which called for that body to join the worldwide study of UFOs. Sir Eric M. Gairy, prime minister of the Caribbean island of Grenada, made a special trip to New York to lead the appeal. According to coverage of his speech in *The New York Times*, Gairy told the UN: 'I have myself seen an unidentified flying object, and I have been overwhelmed by what I have seen.' The prime minister added that he was convinced that UFOs were space vehicles used by 'highly intelligent aliens of extraterrestrial origin.'

The UN has debated the issue several times but has never taken definite action on the question of UFOs.

Dr. Sturrok's survey also added flames to the fire at the First International Conference on the UFO Phenomenon, held in Acapulco, Mexico, in April 1977. Jacques Vallée, a leading French astronomer and UFO researcher attending the conference, told *The New York Times*: 'There is a very high probability that life exists elsewhere in the universe. Why shouldn't there be other civilizations in space, more advanced than our own, capable of coming here?'

## WHAT THE RECORD SHOWS

Members of the American delegation to the conference ended the meeting by calling upon the government of the United States to help their research. William Spaulding of GSW and Dr. J. Allen Hynek, director of CUFOS and an astronomy professor at Northwestern University, led the call for a 'more scientific approach to the problem' to be spearheaded by the American military and scientific communities.

As the demand for a worldwide scientific examination of UFOs increases, so does the number of sightings. On October 25, 1978, the Australian Air Force admitted to members of the press that a young pilot had disappeared without a trace after sighting and pursuing a UFO.

The phenomenon of OVNI (oggetto volante no identificato), which stands for unidentified flying objects, has been particularly strong in Italy, especially since there was a rash of UFO sightings in December 1978. Photographers in Palermo, Sicily, Milan, and other cities in Italy captured on film UFOs shaped like doughnuts. The craft, which gave off green, red, and white lights and had a hole in the center like a doughnut, were seen by dozens of people. A Rome police lieutenant, who saw the vehicles himself, told the Associated Press: 'I saw an enormous beam of green light which disappeared in a north-northwesterly direction.'

During the following month, January 1979, a New Zealand movie camera crew made headlines around the world when it filmed a flight of several UFOs in the skies. Frames of the film were shown on television news programs worldwide and made front pages of newspapers such as *The New York Times*.

All of these recorded sightings and encounters not only give the abductees a talking point, but they also add to the confusion about the issue since there were as many different types of aliens and craft in the last few decades as witnesses describe today. Jessica Rolfe is convinced, based on information she gleaned during her contact with several of them, that there are twelve alien races. Lydia Stalnaker described three kinds after her two abductions, and Travis Walton was positive he had seen two. Alien types similar to those seen by modern abductees were described in the past.

The majority of witnesses have seen the short, oval-headed beings described by the Hills and Walton. Another frequently distinguished type matches Rolfe's *Kuran*– tall, well-proportioned, with a golden or tan tint to their skin.

In other words, the published information gives the abductees a feeling of relief, a sense that they are not alone. They learn that sightings of UFOs and strange humanoids have been reported for centuries, whether real visitations or simply conjured up in the human mind.

One thing that the abductees learn is that they appear to have much in common with the witnesses of the past. In not one case were the extraterrestrials (if that is what they are) cruel to humans, even during attempted abductions.

An incident that occurred in April 1961, just four months before Betty and Barney Hill were captured by humanoids in New Hampshire, is occasionally mentioned by abductees.

In that month, a sixty-year-old farmer in Eagle River, Wisconsin, offered a drink of cool water to the three occupants of a disc-shaped, silver flying craft that landed in his farmyard. According to Coral Lorenzen ('UFO Occupants in the United States,' in *The Humanoids*), the short, oval-headed beings thankfully gave him four small wafers in exchange. Since he had seen the visitors cooking the wafers before they took off at high speed, the farmer assumed they were edible.

He consumed one of the wafers, which he found tasteless, and gave one to NICAP, an independent UFO research group, and one to the air force to study, keeping the fourth as his private souvenir. No report of the contents or consistency was ever released by either group, a matter that will be examined more closely in Chapter Six. Moreover, the farmer did not say that he was abducted or physically examined.

Since many of the abductees had no memory of their capture until undergoing hypnosis or experiencing a delayed recall, it is impossible to say whether the abductions really started with the Hills in 1961 or with Professor Guimaraes in

1957. There could be others who never had the opportunity to uncover their time lapses and just forgot about it or lived with it.

What is important, particularly in the eyes of the witnesses, is that no case is an isolated incident. The evidence that UFOs may be a very old part of earthly records is readily available. Those who study these records suggest there is life on other planets, or, perhaps, unknown races living in secluded pockets of our own earth. Whatever the real source of UFOs, there is no question that the phenomenon has international scope and repercussions.

Chapter Three

# What Will the Neighbors Say?

Once the abductee has become aware of the details of his capture, whether through lengthy hypnosis or sudden recall, the usual response is a period of shock and trauma. The emotional hysteria – the fear experienced at the moment of capture – suddenly surfaces and becomes a very real, present sensation. The abductees may have to live through several weeks or months of adjusting to the memory, the tension, and reawakened fears.

But the time does come when the abductee has adjusted to the experience, accepted it, and begun to try to understand it. Perhaps he has begun reading about other UFO abductions in books or magazines or written to one of the UFO organizations for information. Whatever the abductee has begun to do, one problem is sure to arise in his mind: 'Should I go public? Should I tell my story to the outside world?'

The options are open. The abductee can keep quiet, telling his story only to a few family members and perhaps a trusted friend. Or he can join the handful of abductees who have made their stories known to the public, either of their own volition or by accident. If he chooses the latter course, he must be prepared to face one of the most excruciating periods of his life. Even Dr. James Harder, a professor at the University of California at Berkeley who is director of research for APRO, admits that it is 'sometimes smarter not to go public.'

## WHAT WILL THE NEIGHBORS SAY?

It appears that although most people love to dream and hypothesize about space travel, they are not ready to cope with the possibility of actual visitors from other planets. The abductee considering telling his story to the public need only look at today's television shows to be forewarned about typical attitudes. On a 1974 episode of the short-lived series 'Apple's Way,' the lead character saw what he suspected was a UFO and went public with his story. He was ridiculed and in the end made to feel foolish when it was determined that he had probably seen an experimental weather balloon.

On an episode of the television series 'Soap' in March 1979, Burt Campbell observes a UFO while standing on a country road and faces stinging rejection from his family and friends. On the final episode of the 1978 – 79 television season, millions of viewers saw Burt apparently abducted by the craft before the show faded into summer reruns. How he fared, and if his family believed him, remained to be told in the next season.

The message from the media is clear: seeing a UFO is like saying you've seen a ghost. People will laugh at you. Saying you've been abducted by a UFO is considered even more ludicrous. The person who wants to find out more about UFOs and peruses the shelves at a bookstore finds the material on the subject not in the science or astronomy section but in the occult section alongside books on mediums and palm reading. The books sell well, for interest is high, but another message is clear because books in the occult section are generally considered 'for kooks.'

With these stereotyped images bombarding an already anxious psyche, the abductee must decide which road to take, public or secret, whether to share a very thought-provoking experience or let society debate the UFO controversy with the abductee on the sidelines.

Jessica Rolfe has elected to tell her story only to those who she feels will understand. She says that 'it can be disturbing for some to hear. I have no desire to be on national television with it.' As a silent abductee, she has experienced no reactions in her community. Her mother has been supportive, nonetheless.

'To go public you must be very strong and very together,' says Dr. Iris H. Maack, the Duke University-trained psychologist who specializes in helping abductees cope with their experience. 'I never suggest they go public. If they ask me, "Should I go public?" or "Will it help others if I go public?" then we talk about it. Often the desire to go public is an altruistic one. The abductee feels that he had no one to turn to when he had his experience, and that by going public he can become a sounding board for others.'

The road to becoming public after an abduction is not always direct in some cases. Travis Walton had been missing for more than five days. When he was found he was already news, with local and wire-service reporters following searchers, demanding an explanation for where he had been. Since there were six witnesses to his encounter with a strange craft, the community already knew that a UFO was supposed to be involved. Walton didn't have a choice; he had to explain his abduction, to stand with courage and let the community react as it would.

For the most part, the other abductees had the option of choosing when and how they would go public. 'We didn't go public actually,' explains Betty Hill, echoing Walton's experience to some degree. 'An investigative reporter heard a version of the abduction at a party. He put the pieces together by interviewing people in Portsmouth (New Hampshire) and all of a sudden we opened the paper and there it was.' The Hills had to decide whether to just let the story, which had many inaccuracies, stand and try to ignore the response or go public with their version.

The Hills had wanted to keep the experience to themselves and had confided in family and some friends and a UFO group. Still, once the story was out in the open the strong-willed Hills were not about to move out of town. They came forth with the complete story and were ready to face whatever reaction the community might offer.

Several of the abductees readily told their stories. Charles Hickson and Calvin Parker, the Mississippi abductees, debated the question for a few hours and then decided that the public should be told that there were alien beings capable of visiting us. They voluntarily told their experiences to the police and the media. Carl Higdon, who had his adventure in Wyoming, had no qualms about going public immediately, and Jeffrey Greenhaw, the Alabaman, took a similar position.

Greenhaw knew what he had seen; he even had four Polaroid photographs that proved, as far as he was concerned, that he had indeed encountered a spaceman. As police often do, he shared his most interesting findings of the evening, including the unique photographs, with the local newspaper. The citizenry should be told, he mused, that this creature was, in fact, in the vicinity. He was doing his duty, never suspecting the possibility of negative consequences.

After wrestling with the emotional and physical trauma of their group abduction for several days, Mona Stafford made an appointment with her physician in the hope of curing the severe burning sensation in her eyes still remaining from the night of her abduction in Kentucky. The doctor told her he had recently read an article about Hickson and Parker, of whose abduction Stafford was completely unaware. The physician convinced her that it was her duty to report such an experience. He also agreed with her assessment of her own personality. Stafford was convinced that it would help her feel better about the abduction if she could discuss it openly and try to warn others.

Stafford telephoned Smith and Thomas, who were with her at the time, but they were opposed to 'going public.' Louise Smith was particularly adamant because she feared she would lose her job if word got out. Stafford rejected their arguments. 'I decided that people have to know about it,' she explains. 'They may not want to know about it, but they'd better. It's important.'

Sometimes no matter how much a public service the abductee may feel he is performing when he shares the story, the very act of allowing publicity may lead to ridicule or accusations that the contactee is trying to perpetrate a hoax.

Such was the result for Jeffrey Greenhaw. His superiors and the entire community came down on him to retract his statement. 'They wanted me to deny it, to say it wasn't true, but I knew it was,' he remembers bitterly. 'I had to leave the state of Alabama for an indefinite period.'

His former 'buddies' were even more persuasive than his bosses. They took matters into their own hands. Greenhaw's trailer was burned down. Soon after, his wife divorced him, partly, he believes, because she couldn't bear to be associated with his name and the ridicule.

'Maybe my wife and I had had it without this,' Greenhaw said to us. 'But I still was able to see things clearly when I lost her support. As for the rest of the community, I didn't expect it. I didn't expect six men – and I know who they were – to come and burn my house to the ground just to get me out of town.

'I had grown up with these people,' he continues, his bitterness apparent. 'I was not a saint, but I was one of them. That didn't seem to matter, I guess. You should have heard what the ladies at church said – and they're supposed to be Christian people.'

Greenhaw's experience might be considered the negative end of the scale. He contends that the violent reaction may have something to do with living in a rural area or even in the South. Dr. Harder and Dr. Maack, the UFO scholars, agree that the more rural the area, the more difficult it is for the public abductee. According to Dr. Maack, 'The rural areas are less tolerant and seem to have a greater fear of aliens as well as technology itself. I'm from the South, but I have to admit that the abductees here have the worst time. The pattern seems to be that the more urban you are, the less trouble you have.'

'I'd like to think it was more or less the area,' Greenhaw admits. 'Because I've been in touch with some nice people in the western and northwestern parts of this country. In this area I have lived nearly all my life. I went to school with them.

Everyone knows me. They trusted me enough to make me police chief. They know I wouldn't say something happened if it didn't. And they still don't want to believe it.'

It would be incorrect to assume that Jeffrey Greenhaw's case sets any standards even for the rural abductees. Despite Louise Smith's fears, the experience of Mona Stafford and Elaine Thomas, who also lived in the rural Liberty area of Kentucky, was not as unfortunate, although it also was frightening.

'When our story first spread around the area, more people didn't believe than believed,' Louis Smith recalls. 'It was not a happy period for me; there were many critical remarks.'

'There were some people going around asking "Have you seen any little green men lately?"' Mona Stafford adds, 'I'd tell them that I never said I had seen little green men and that nobody had ever seen little green men. I'd say, you can laugh if you want to, I used to be like you. I'd tell them they could laugh, but it might not be so funny one of these days. Of course, not everyone was like that. If they had been, we would have killed ourselves.'

Smith, Stafford, and Thomas, who died in 1978, had many rough months. Dr. R. Leo Sprinkle, the psychologist who has been researching UFOs for twenty-five years and conducted the hypnoses of the three women, recalls receiving many telephone calls from them at his office at the University of Wyoming, Laramie. Each time they would sound nervous, seeking aid and answers. Yet throughout he was secure in the knowledge that their psychological profiles were better than he might have expected. He knew they could cope.

Stafford also remembers that period and her need to seek advice from any quarter.

'I had to have help,' she says, emotions still high. 'I needed someone to listen to me and try to understand. My mother was there for me. I'd tell her how it would make me feel depressed and useless when someone didn't believe me, and real angry if they laughed. Sometimes it was pitiful. But it's just their ignorance. There should be no place for ignorance.'

As the pressures of Liberty became more intense, Smith and Stafford fled to other states, hoping to find some peace. Smith moved to Las Vegas, Nevada, where she lives today as the manager of a Mexican restaurant. Stafford moved to Stanford, Kentucky, not far from the site of the abduction, then shifted to Florida. She found she missed her family and cautiously returned to Kentucky. She now lives in Dunnville, near Liberty.

'It's been hard to make friends,' Stafford insists. 'The abduction is something they just don't want to talk about. But I have to talk about it whether they like it or not, even if it means people aren't going to like me for it. They are either my friends, or not, that's the way I feel. I'd rather have one good friend, than one thousand.'

Travis Walton, who had his adventure in Arizona, has also found the path a rough one. 'I don't think other people can understand,' he asserts today. 'Because without really having been through it I couldn't understand either. On the other hand, they have been understanding about it and the way I treat the experience. I don't let it interfere with my life. I think I've handled it pretty good.

'Very little negative has been said to my face, but I know some things were said behind my back,' he continues. 'It wasn't an outward thing, really, nothing violent. It's just little things. Like, we went skating once and I fell several times. I could hear people whispering that I was awkward and falling because I was wild, I had a wild look in my eyes, or I was drunk. For awhile people would come up to me and expect me to have antennae on my head. But all that died down.'

Yet both Walton and Charles Hickson have been the subject of character assassinations. Unrelated incidents from their past were revived in efforts to discredit them.

Attempts were made to discredit Hickson's honesty by pointing to the fact that he had declared bankruptcy several months prior to the abduction, but since he has recorded no financial gains from his experience, he regards this as a shallow charge. Similarly, an incident in Walton's youth – when he was found guilty of passing a bad check – was used to his disfavor even though he had made full restitution. Rumors began as people recalled and embellished his 'criminal record' despite promises that the files were supposed to have been sealed. In virtually every attack, his youth at the time of the misdeed and the fact that he had made full restitution immediately were not mentioned.

'We lost our jobs after the incident,' recalls Walton, who does not seem cut out for the public eye. 'I've found it difficult to get work, the choices of employment have been limited. I can't say it's because of my publicity, but I'm sure that's taken into account when someone is making a decision about hiring.'

Carl Higdon feels he has faced little negative reaction. His home town of Rawlins, Wyoming, is not unlike Walton's community in Snowflake, Arizona, in that both are small, camaraderie is a natural part of life, and both towns are distant from a large city. Higdon found that after he went public, many neighbors began telling him their own personal stories of alien contacts.

'After I told people and they read it in the papers they just said, "Yeah, there's been some awful weird things goin' on down south of Rawlins," Higdon recalls. 'I'll tell you, most of the people around here are coal miners or they work in the oil fields or they're ranchers. And these ranchers, they see a lot of stuff and they talk to us people.

'See, I've done better than other people who've been picked up because around here they know I'm telling the truth. The ranchers see lots of stuff that the public never finds out about. There's many people around here that's seen UFOs in the sky. And we know they're UFOs because we don't get many airplanes and no airplane flies the way these things do. When you see a bright object going across the sky at a very high speed and then it suddenly stops dead and sits there for awhile before continuing at high speed, you know it's not an airplane.'

Local lore has it that odd things have happened before in

the dense forest area that Higdon had used for hunting. Higdon says he knows of an abductee who has never gone public living nearby, a woman who had an experience with aliens identical to his but dared not come forward with her story.

This is not to say that Higdon has gone unscathed. After his abduction, rumors circulated that he was 'freaked out' on narcotics when his experience occurred. Those who know Higdon were aware that he did not use narcotics, and he rarely drank anything alcoholic. His wife says she has only seen him drunk once in twenty-one years, his friends have seen him drink at most an occasional Tom Collins, and he had not been drinking that day.

'If people don't believe me, I invite them to my house,' says the affable, likable Higdon. 'I show them letters from researchers, and I show them clippings about other abductions.

'Sometimes they still don't believe me. So I'll tell them, "Okay, you explain how my pickup truck got stuck in a mudhole. You tell me why I would take a two-wheel drive pickup into an area that four-wheel trucks have trouble with." They can't answer that. They know I wouldn't do anything that crazy.'

Ellecia Gruen, the Michigan homemaker who had observed UFOs before, has also found it beneficial to confront her detractors face to face.

'I'm known as the UFO lady here in Ogden Center and I'm highly respected,' she insists. 'But that doesn't mean that everyone has that respect. All those who want to criticize me are invited over to my house. Then after they've met me they have the right to form an opinion. And everybody that's come over has never harassed me afterward. I've never turned anybody away from calling or coming over. They can even go to the area where a lot of this happened.'

Gruen has been fortunate to retain the support of her friends throughout her ordeal. In the early 1970s when she first remembered the encounter, they never suggested she was mentally ill or should seek professional help. Instead, they offered their opinions on whether there was life on other planets and let the subject run its course.

Later, in 1976, these friends remained by her side during the three-month ordeal. They became witnesses to the UFOs flying overhead, to the poltergeist in her home. They saw Gruen grow depressed and lose weight. They saw her two German shepherds cowering in corners of her home. It was never the neighbors that upset Gruen.

'I just couldn't understand what was going on,' she says today. 'My friends couldn't help there. No one could answer my questions. I called a planetarium, but the man there could not explain the UFOs. I called the Federal Aviation Administration, but they sort of laughed me off. I didn't know whom to contact. You just don't look in the telephone book under UFO investigators. That to me was the horror, not being able to explain why all this was going on.'

Lydia Stalnaker, the Florida abductee, had similar frustration before she underwent hypnosis and recalled the details of her abductions; there was no place to turn for help. A self-described 'loner,' she had few friends to lend her support, and her family was also convinced she was in need of immediate professional help.

'I was going crazy, I couldn't stand it anymore.' She describes her emotional state with her characteristic fervor and enthusiasm, 'I thought I was working too hard. My family also thought I was cracking up. They suggested I go to a mental health clinic. I went to one in Sarasota (Florida), but they couldn't find anything wrong, although they found my story about being with that man and looking for the hovering craft, then having a time lapse – they found it all strange.

'So they put me into group therapy with these women who were having dreams about rape and about men chasing them with knives, as if my voices in the night were the same thing. My voices were telling me to become physically fit, not raped. The therapists just wanted me to be like them so they could think they were doing their job. They almost made me crazy. I got out of there.'

Afterwards she decided to give hypnosis a try. Two years later, in 1976, she went public accidentally when the local newspaper stumbled upon her story through bits and pieces heard secondhand. Since then, she has found most of her neighbors to be open-minded but cautious.

'Since the whole thing came out the doctors want to talk to me and they say they understand,' Stalnaker reflects without bitterness but certainly with some annoyance at their Johnny-come-lately attitude. 'Before they said it couldn't be true, now suddenly I'm not crazy anymore. As to the people, well I've got friends, but I'm not really close to many. Sometimes it seems they want to know me because of all this, like I'm a curiosity. That upsets me more than ridicule would. I feel they should like me because of myself, not because I'm in the newspapers.'

Stalnaker rejects the idea of inviting those who ridicule to her home in the manner of Gruen. 'I'm not interested in people visiting. I don't want a bunch of people coming over here because they want to get very close and be part of my private life. They want to know all about me, like I'm public property. Do you know that people will sometimes comment that they're surprised I look normal? Did they expect me to look like a monster? Of course I look normal!'

All the abductees admit that when they first went public, people would point them out on the streets or be more direct and approach them, wanting to know all the details of the encounter. Mona Stafford, the Kentucky woman, was a bit overwhelmed. 'When it first happened the phone was constantly busy and I told the story over and over,' she remembers. 'I told it so much that I began to feel I was beating my head against the wall with most people. I finally got to where I was watching them from the very beginning just to see if they were sincere or if they saw me as a curiosity.'

The initial excitement has died down for the abductees

now, and they go about the routines of their daily lives much as they did before the incidents. For many, however, the feeling of sometimes being social outcasts remains.

'People are always coming up to me and asking if I'm the one,' says Betty Hill, who has had fifteen years to develop a sense of humor over the situation. 'I say yes, I'm the one, but I didn't commit a murder or anything.'

Betty and Barney Hill were well known in Portsmouth for their work in civil rights and in the Unitarian church. Following Barney's death in 1969, Betty has remained active and a respected and beloved member of the community. It has been suggested that the positive reaction they received was due to the age-old New England tradition of honoring local eccentrics, something apparent in essays and other writings about the region. But there was nothing eccentric about the couple. Surely, since theirs was an interracial marriage, they had come under public scrutiny years before their abduction. Yet their political and community work made them welcome in most Portsmouth circles. It was Betty and Barney Hill who represented Portsmouth at the inauguration of Lyndon B. Johnson as president of the United States even before the abduction became public knowledge. And during one of his campaigns in New Hampshire, Nelson Rockefeller sent Barney a personal greeting.

Perhaps because of their already established credibility, the Hills found more believers than disbelievers among the people who contacted them after the abduction became national news. Others among the known abductees have not fared as well.

While Hickson and Parker received thousands of letters and phone calls, the vast majority supportive, Mona Stafford felt a mixed reaction. 'If people ask me about it and I tell them, I don't get anything out of it, I do it for them,' says the soft-spoken, attractive woman. 'I find that about one-third of those that ask are sincerely interested and it's easy to explain it to them. Then another third of the people don't believe and they make you frustrated because they refuse to listen. But the worst is the last group. About one-third of the people who ask about the abduction want to talk to you just to get a laugh. I get so depressed because they're just plain ignorant and cruel and there just isn't any place for ignorance like that.'

All of the abductees are aware of those who scoff at them or have elected to keep their distance, but the contactees appear to have drawn strength from the ostracism, choosing, like Mona Stafford, to expand their own outlooks and appreciate their own inner qualities. Thus, despite the handful of horror stories like Jeffrey Greenhaw's, the public abductees have fared relatively well in their communities.

What often bothers them more is the lack of privacy that comes with any degree of recognition and fame. Most continue to receive large numbers of letters and phone calls, some of which are anything but complimentary. Louise Smith and Charles Hickson have unlisted telephone numbers. Travis Walton has no phone, primarily to protect the privacy of his family.

'My telephone number leaks out and people from all over the country call at different times of the day or night,' Hickson reports. 'I've had people calling me here in Gautier (Mississippi) from Canada, California and everywhere else, often in the middle of the night. Somehow they get my phone number. Generally, it's not to ridicule me; they usually just want to ask questions. But I don't need that, so I have to change my telephone number quite often.'

Louise Smith also has frequently changed her unlisted number in an attempt to protect her privacy. Mona Stafford is on a party line and does sometimes receive inquiring phone calls, but she is very cautious about answering them. 'My neighbors just don't understand,' she told us. 'So it doesn't do any good for someone to phone me, I never answer questions on the telephone because others can listen in.'

Often, the telephone calls and letters serve as a source of widespread psychological support for the abductees. Betty Hill spends many hours each week answering letters, all at her own expense. When the Hills first went public, Betty and Barney even hired an answering service so they wouldn't miss anyone's message. Calls come from as far away as Europe.

'At first we were sorry we went public because it was costing us a fortune,' she says, laughing. 'All the postage, typing paper and typewriter ribbons began to add up.'

The vast majority of the Hills' mail has always been very positive. 'Obscene calls? Oh, no, we didn't get them,' Betty insists. 'No one attacked us. After all, we were involved with things much more controversial than UFOs,' she adds, alluding to her interracial marriage.

Lydia Stalnaker, who reported being abducted in Florida, is less pleased with her letters, which have come steadily over the years. She is particularly bothered not by people who want to attack her but by those claiming to be comrades. Some say they are reincarnated aliens or have been abducted to Venus. Lydia feels she has inadvertently attracted some fringe elements in society.

'I'm sick of all this stuff, and I get letters all the time,' she complains. 'Half of them are nuts. They say, "Will you please tell the aliens to give me a million dollars." Real trash. And I sit here and laugh, but I feel a bit sorry for them.

'I mean they get crazier. They'll write and say, "I live in such and such a place and I want the aliens to drop by and pay a visit," and they're serious. Then there are the ones who say, "Listen, when you leave with the aliens next time would you please tell me so I can go with you." I keep my sense of humor about this. I guess they think I'm on a first-name basis with them up there.'

On many occasions support comes through these calls and letters as well or just through being out with the rest of the community. One time, a woman walked up to Stalnaker with some information that brought tears to her eyes, confirming in her own mind that she was not herself disturbed, that her experience must have been real.

'Even after the hypnosis it took a long time for me to really believe that it happened,' she admits, always direct with herself and with interviewers. 'I always wanted to think I was dreaming. Maybe under hypnosis I had made up a story. I suppose I knew the abduction was real, but it seems so far out that you search for another explanation.

'Then once after I had spoken on the subject, my sister introduced me to a woman she said had wanted to meet me for a long time, but had been too shy. Turns out this woman was coming out of a church and she saw a hovering UFO, maybe the same one I did. It was not more than 150 feet from this rural church. She rushed back into the church and the people came out and they watched. They say it hovered for two hours, then shot off. It was the same place, the same day, the same time that I had my encounter.

'You can't imagine how good that made me feel,' she says, still excited. 'I thought, thank God, other people had seen it, a whole bunch of people. It took four years before anybody came forward and said it. For four years, I stood very much alone.'

Carl Higdon gets letters similar to those received by Stalnaker, and, like her, he takes them with grace and a sense of humor.

'I got this one crank letter,' Higdon says, laughing. 'This ol' boy said he heard that the aliens were coming down soon, and that if I had any teen-age daughters or other relatives he'd appreciate me getting in touch with him. I think he's kinda a weirdo. It's just good that people like that don't show up in person.'

Ellecia Gruen welcomes contact with other people, especially if they have questions about their own sightings. She feels that she can offer some security and support to those who have had an encounter or just seen a UFO. She recalls that when she had her experience there was no one to turn to for help.

'They can write to me, if the people have questions or just want to get something out of their system,' she insists. 'I guess it gives them hope to know that someone has got a big enough mouth to come forward and say she has seen something. People have sightings and they're afraid – afraid that they'll be ridiculed, or that something is wrong with them inside. I try to explain what's going on. If they are sincere, they can write to me as long and as often as they'd like to.'

Gruen has received many letters but none that she'll show publicly. Like the investigators, she will not discuss individual cases, honoring the concept of confidentiality. If she hears from a correspondent who wants to go public, she will refer reporters to them.

Betty Hill has found that many persons come to her with information about sightings and questions. By having gone public, she seems to be serving a central purpose, standing alone as someone who can be trusted by people who desperately seek someone with understanding to speak with.

'I don't get laughed at,' Betty says. 'I get the opposite reaction more often. I tell what happened to us and people get pensive, then offer me their stories. They say, "You're the spokesman for us."

'I have this happen everyday. Last summer a well-known judge said a UFO landed between his house and his barn. His whole family stood in the windows and watched. Then they called Pease Air Force Base, which sent someone out to question them. And the judge told me about it. He said, "Look, I can't go on TV and say I had a UFO land in my backyard, but *you* can go on TV and say that you know someone who had a UFO land in his backyard."'

That has not been an isolated incident for her. If other residents of New Hampshire spot a UFO or have other spectacular sightings, they'll pick up the phone and call her; she has never had an unlisted number. Often the calls come from someone who was told by someone else to contact her. One morning, a man saw a UFO land. He went to church later that day and sheepishly confided in the minister and others. They all said, 'Call Betty Hill!' He did. Betty Hill jokes that the word is out, 'Don't tell it to God, tell it to Betty Hill.'

'I've had people come up to me and say, "I'd like to say you're crazy,"' Hill relates. 'Then they pause and add, "If the same thing happens to me, I'm going to need you."'

While some people have tried to harass Louise Smith and Mona Stafford, others came to them to share stories of bizarre sightings, usually of the large animal or man-ape they call Big Foot in Kentucky. Several neighbors have insisted that Stafford accompany them to the site of their encounter, pointing out animal bones or other residue as 'proof' that a carnivorous beast was, in fact, in the area. Stafford usually complies and has found herself growing interested and increasingly curious about the nature of what they have seen. It leads her to speculation as much as her own abduction does.

Any strange phenomenon appears to fall into the category of problems brought to the UFO abductees by their neighbors. The consensus seems to be that they will be able to understand or at least empathize. In this way, it is clear that despite minor harassment, the abductees have, indeed, achieved a level of respect within their communities, perhaps precisely because they spoke out and have weathered negative feedback. In some cases, their firmness has earned them a position in the communities that they previously lacked. In terms of UFOs or other unusual happenings, they are the local 'elders,' the wise men able to dole out advice and comfort.

Unquestionably, they have, even in their own minds, achieved some measure of respect simply by their courage to stand up for what they believe. All the abductees speak of people who 'came around' after a while; that is, they came to accept the validity of the abduction from the abductee's point of view even if they still did not embrace the idea of UFOs. With the exception of Jeffrey Greenhaw, no abductee has been forced to leave the town in which he lived. Some, however, have decided to move independently of local pressure.

Others, such as Charles Hickson, have lost touch with longtime friends, separating themselves from the past. We telephoned one self-described 'old buddy' of Hickson's in an early attempt to track down the abductee. The man resided in Pascagoula, Mississippi, but was not aware that Hickson was still living nearby in Gautier. They had no contact for some time, and the old friend did not know any people who had been in touch with Hickson. He indicated that Hickson had left the state of Mississippi, showing how little he knew about his old friend since the abduction incident.

Mona Stafford and Louise Smith, who became close friends after the abduction, although they had barely known each other before, have since lost touch. Smith explained that she still writes to family and friends in Kentucky but lost Stafford's address somehow during the many moves the two women had made. She didn't seem to have made a serious effort to track Stafford down, and vice versa. There is no animosity between the women, just a desire not to feel the immediacy of the abduction again.

Still, despite good times and bad times, because of the small number of public abductees, they must stand alone wherever they reside. Dr. Iris Maack, the psychologist, points to them as 'role models for future public abductees,' but it is not easy to find patterns or common ground in the nature of their experiences. In most cases, the doors of the community are open if they wish to assimilate again, but, by nature alone, it is not possible for them to blend back in their home towns after the trauma they have been through.

That most of the public abductees continue to speak with some regularity on the subject is evidence that they feel no need to retreat from their frequently challenged positions. They continue to appear on television and radio talk shows and welcome interviewers and interested parties into their homes. They stand on no soap boxes; they merely say what they feel must be said. After all, they are not trained public speakers, they note, just citizens trying to alert others to a strange event.

**DIRECT ENCOUNTERS**

It is not clear why these people chose to go public or remain in the public eye. For some, like Greenhaw, it appeared to be part of their duty. For others, the feeling that they could help others was the motivation. Other contactees cannot clearly define a reason, just as they cannot fully explain the abduction. Going public may lead to understanding, but testimonial dinners are a long way off.

## Chapter Four

# Family Loyalty

Many abductees do not publicize their experiences; they only tell researchers because the reaction of neighbors, friends and relatives usually is a mixed bag, and going public may lead to anxiety that is uncomfortable in itself.

Some do not confide in their families, either fearing that they could become vulnerable at home or hoping to save their children and spouse from public ridicule. An abduction not only changes lives, it affects family relationships.

Jeffrey Greenhaw learned the hard way that 'until death do us part' is not an unbreakable vow. He had been experiencing problems in his marriage before his experience, but he thought it could survive.

'Things weren't going well there,' he admits today, resigned to the fact that his talk about an encounter with aliens played a role in his divorce. 'But after the incident it was all clearer to me. I was able to detect things in the marriage that my eyes had been blind to. There was no support when I went public about the experience. The criticism came in from around me and I was standing alone. Maybe if I retracted my statement and was quiet it would have been different, but I couldn't.

'We got a divorce. Maybe we had had it without the encounter and the rest, maybe not. Those pictures [of the alien] sure did make a difference in our relationship, though.'

Greenhaw's negative experience is probably not representative, but it is the fear that something like this will happen that keeps many abductees silent in their own homes, the memory of the experience bottled up. Afraid to turn to their families for support, witnesses double their anxiety and increasingly need a release, a means to unburden their reactions to the encounter to a sympathetic person. A confidant must be found.

For such situations, there are psychologists who specialize in helping abductees, such as Dr. Iris Maack of Savannah, Georgia, who has lent her ear and given guidance to some of them. A psychologist with an interest in studying the effects of extreme stress, such as a UFO encounter, she finds herself upset by the fact that abductees frequently cannot bring themselves to at least confide in their wives, children, and parents.

'Quite a few have not discussed it with their families even after receiving counsel from us,' Dr. Maack told us. 'They are fearful of the reactions they will receive from them; after all, sometimes the approval of our families is what we cherish most. Secondly, they want to protect their families from ridicule and I guess they figure in the long run it is better if no one knows. I imagine that families become suspicious that something is bothering the individual and that after a while the secrecy does damage to the family unit.'

Although there is no simple answer to the problem, the concerns of the abductees generally prove to be unwarranted. Most of the witnesses' families have fared remarkably well, experiencing, at worst, a neutral response from the neighbors. In any event, negative cases are not the rule.

Of course, the abductees do not necessarily fit into the 'normal' family pattern of wife, husband, and two children, nor is the family always excluded from the contact. Ellecia Gruen was an orphan, so she did not have to worry about telling her parents. Her sons and husband were in the same house and watched the daily UFO flybys with her; it was a family event. Mona Stafford was a self-supporting divorcee trying to raise a sometimes rebellious teenage boy. Louise Smith was a widow with grown children. Jessica Rolfe was an adopted child with an adoptive older sister. Travis Walton was single. Barney and Betty Hill were an interracial couple with no children of their own, although Barney's sons did visit often and were fond of Betty.

Carl Higdon, who reported only negligible negative reaction from his community and friends, says proudly that his family is as close as ever. His wife, Margery, remembers vividly the fateful evening when he was abducted since she kept a worrisome vigil with friends waiting for word of her husband's recovery.

When he was found, she rushed to the forest preserve with the friends, relieved that her husband was safe. On the way, she reported seeing an odd, glowing craft with green and white lights, which she believed was a UFO, moving rapidly away from the area in which Carl had been hunting. When Higdon did tell his story, she became his most vocal supporter, standing at his side as she had for all their married life. The Higdons admit that their four children may have heard unpleasant remarks in school from time to time but shrug and say, 'You know how children can be.' There has never been an instance when any of the children has come home tearful or with clothes torn after a fight. Family life is as it was, with Higdon a strong and loving head of the household and his wife slightly more prone to give in to the children.

In fact, abducted parents can sometimes become a status symbol to children and grandchildren. Lydia Stalnaker, who at the time of her abduction was divorced and raising two daughters, explained that her daughters have faced different reactions, but to the younger girl she is a mother the other children want to meet.

'She brings then around,' Stalnaker says, laughing. 'They want to see me. I think they think it is great. My daughter is very interested in what I have to say about the abductions and she even wishes something like it could happen to her. She has pride in me, and it's a good feeling for her to know that her friends think her mama is something special, too.

'But see,' she says somberly, 'with different age groups it

goes another way. My older daughter does not want to hear anything about my experiences and I can see why. When this all came out the kids in her school were cruel. They would come up to her and ask if she was the girl with the "space mama." My younger one likes the expression "space mama." The older one gets angry whenever it is mentioned.'

Ellecia Gruen's older son had a very difficult time of it when she saw alien spacecraft buzzing around her house in 1976. In Gruen's words, 'Everyone knew I was seeing them. He was ridiculed by his friends. His grades dropped because he was seeing the UFOs, too, and was disturbed by them as much as I was. He went from As and Bs at school to Cs and Ds. There was little we could do about it except continue to love him. You see, in my case my experiences also belong to my family. They are part of it.' Today, the younger son, who was, at the time of the encounter, in diapers and crib, encourages his mother to speak of the time the UFOs came. The older boy ignores it as much as possible but is still close to his mother.

'When I first had the memory of the encounter in the orphanage my husband thought it was a dream,' Gruen recalls. 'When I persisted in saying that I knew it was not, he suggested I see a psychiatrist or seek some sort of professional help. I don't know if he really believed the aliens had examined me by my bed.

'Of course, there was no question that the UFOs in 1976 were real, even to him. He sort of got tired of me talking to reporters for no money. I got the feeling that he was trying to run my life and we have separated. Without these UFOs I suppose we would still be together, but what is, is.'

It appears as though the concern of abductees that their families will reject them is unfounded. True, Jeffrey Greenhaw's wife did divorce him, and the Gruens have separated, but, by their own admission, that was not because of the encounters but because they insisted on going public.

Louise Smith, one of the three women involved in the Kentucky incident, is happy to say that her daughter 'has always been there when I needed her throughout this. She was the one I turned to, the one who kept me going.'

Smith moved to Las Vegas where she can have greater control over whom she does and does not see, and her small circle of friends know her as a warm and good-hearted neighbor. Her daughter, son, their spouses, and three grandchildren all appear proud of her, as she, in turn, speaks with pride about her five-year-old grandson, who has seen her on television and often asks her questions about UFOs and other planets.

'He can discuss it with the best of them and I don't tell him what to say.' She beams proudly. 'He's picked up so much knowledge and interest. I'm glad about that. And I'm glad that it gives him a thrill to see his grandma being interviewed on television.'

Her coabductee does not share her euphoria about the reaction of the children. Mona Stafford sadly admits that she is having problems communicating with her son Greg partly because of his need to exert his independence but, she insists, also because of the abduction publicity and the changes in the way she lives her life.

Greg now lives with his father. Stafford rarely sees him, which is a source of pain to her.

'I don't think he quite knows how to take me anymore,' she confides. 'I think it hurts him a lot. I was always so serious and responsibility was so important to me. Before this happened to me, art, religion and being a mother—those were my interests in life. My duties before all things were going to church and my home. I was having problems with him because he was a teenager and you know how teenagers are today. But my family was my life. After this happened I changed. I'm less strict. I run around more having fun.'

As a result, Stafford sees less of Greg than she used to, and she misses the contact and feeling of family love. Not once did she imply that Greg's estrangement was due to the abduction or what others might have said about the abduction. It is her personality change and the resultant altering of their relationship that may have unnerved him.

Stafford's father has also been less understanding of her situation, but she takes his attitude much more philosophically. 'Dad just doesn't want to believe it,' she explains. 'He knows something happened, but he doesn't want to know. He wants to close his eyes to it, if you know what I mean. He's the type that if he saw a UFO himself, he wouldn't want to believe it.'

For his part, her father, Edward Witt, sounds ambivalent. He still lives in Liberty, Kentucky, and receives frequent visits from his daughter while keeping a watchful eye on her activities. Since he is easier to reach than Stafford, reporters often speak to him before they can locate her. He is cordial but tries to dissuade interest and publicity, no doubt because of his concern for his daughter.

'What I want to do is forget about it,' he reluctantly told us. 'I think the less she talks about it the better off she'll be.'

However skeptical Witt may be about Stafford's experience, he has always been a devoted, caring parent. When she was experiencing stress and anxiety, suffering from the shock of the capture for almost a year after the event, Witt and his wife Mary, who died in 1977, welcomed their child back into their home to recuperate.

'I was so frightened I wouldn't sleep without a light,' Stafford remembers. 'Lots of times I'd hear a peck or two on the window and I'd jump up and run out like a little kid. Here I was 35 years old and I'd stand in front of my parents' bedroom door. Fortunately, Mom was a light sleeper and she'd get up and tend me.'

There are tears in Stafford's eyes today as she recalls how her mother helped see her through those terribly rough days. 'If it hadn't been for her I guess I would have cracked up,' she adds with a grateful smile.

Mrs. Witt died of cancer in March of 1977, but if her daughter is thankful for any part of her abduction experience, it is that she was closer to her mother for the last year of her life than she had ever been to any person. Daily, she would pour out the innermost feelings on to her mother's shoulder, repeating not only the events of January 6, 1976, but all aspects of her life. As is frequently the case during periods of such intimacy, it was only natural for Mrs. Witt to soothe her daughter's frail nerves by speaking quite frankly about herself, too.

'Because of my experience Mom could tell me things that she had been keeping inside herself,' Stafford says, her composure returned. 'She told me that she had seen a large, weird being that she called "Big Foot." She had seen it. Mom never said anything unless it was the way it was, she didn't tell stories or lies. I'm not just saying that because she was my mother. You can ask anybody and they'll tell you what type of person and Christian she was.

'She said she had seen this creature out in the garden and it was standing on two feet and two legs and it looked as big as a bear, but she knew it was no bear. We teased her about it at the time, saying it had escaped from a zoo, so she didn't talk about it again until it happened to me. She was thinking she'd help me by telling me the story, but I think it might have helped her, too, because she explained to me how frightened and scared she had been, to be alone in the house all the time knowing that thing was around here.'

Mrs. Witt recalled that she watched as the tall creature walked three steps and vanished into thin air. Whether her daughter believed this really did happen is irrelevant, the repetition of the event was therapeutic to both of them.

Jeffrey Greenhaw extracts a sense of strength and pride by reporting, 'My parents told people who said bad things about my encounter to go to hell.'

The senior Greenhaws live in Hartselle, Alabama, approximately ten miles from Falkville, where Jeffrey had been police chief. As the news spread, his parents also felt the ridicule of area residents and pain because their son was being criticized.

'We're a small family,' Jeffrey explains. 'What happens to one, happens to all. We've got each other always. It has been that way as long as I can remember. There was no way I could lie to them or they not believe that I was telling the truth. And they weren't going to put up with anything from people who didn't have good to say.'

Travis Walton also found that his mother has become his greatest protector. She suffered while he was missing for those 126 hours, and she has vicariously felt his pain. Like Edward Witt, she tries to shield her son and his young family from outsiders. Walton has no telephone of his own, and calls for him are directed to his mother.

It is not unusual for her to try to discourage would-be interviewers and UFO researchers, saying that Walton would rather put the experience behind him. She remarks that the family considers the experience an unfortunate one and calls it 'the disaster.'

Walton does not share the negative feelings his mother expresses but understands that what she says is a reflection of her concern for him.

'When it happened she had to wait until they found me, probably thinking the worst had become of me,' he says. 'Any mother wants to protect her child. In my case there was such a tremendous amount of upset and a lot of vicious things were said about me. They dug up my whole life history and ridiculed me. She didn't like seeing me hurt and always had an eye out to prevent it from recurring.'

The Walton family as a whole deserves to be lauded for the protection and guidance they gave to Travis after he was found on the road outside Heber. Since he had been gone for five days, many newspapermen were on the scene along with the official search party. When Travis came to his senses, he found a telephone booth and called his brother and brother-in-law to come for him. The local authorities still had many questions, but his brother spirited him away so he could avoid the barrage of queries until he had eaten and rested.

As Walton relates in his book *The Walton Experience*, his brother Duane wanted him to receive a physical examination, so he screened doctors until he was sure the abductee would get the proper treatment. In one instance, a hypnotist's office was, in Duane's estimation, filthy, and he pulled his younger brother out. Walton was in no shape to make these decisions for himself.

Obviously an extremely close and self-sufficient group, the entire family pitched in to find places where he could rest and hide from the press until he was ready to talk. For weeks after the abduction, whenever Walton was interviewed by reporters or the sheriff's office—it didn't matter which—one of his brothers was there as a guard and for comfort and support.

Walton had been dating a girl named Dana, and she stuck by him through the roughest parts of readjustment, even when he was in no shape to return her affection. They were married about a year later and now have a son, Clifton. Dana Walton has never expressed any doubt that her husband's explanation for his disappearance is the absolute truth. Like Travis, she would like the incident put behind them so they can get on with living their life together.

Calvin Parker's parents, who live in Laurel, Mississippi, have also been supportive, taking him into their home to recuperate from the trauma of the abduction.

Charles Hickson is particularly proud of a letter he received from one of his sons, who was in the armed forces when he learned of the abduction in the newspaper. The letter expresses the opinion that if Hickson said he was abducted, it must be so because he has never lied. Hickson cherishes the correspondence.

Several of the abductees have been helped in their dealings with family members by the interesting coincidence that others also have seen UFOs. In the case of Lydia Stalnaker, for example, relatives were silent abductees.

When Stalnaker was abducted as a child, she was not taken alone. Her brother and sister, also youngsters at the time, were captured with her. Her brother died in an automobile accident a few years ago, and her sister has refused to undergo hypnosis to reveal the details of her encounter. She told Dr. James Harder, UFO researcher at the University of California at Berkeley, that she was not interested in 'going through what Lydia has gone through.' To the best of Stalnaker's knowledge, her sister has not had any subsequent incidents.

One of the first things Betty Hill thought of the day after their abduction was that her two sisters had seen UFOs in central New Hampshire a few years before. She felt safe, therefore, in discussing their sighting with her family even though 'what they had seen had no resemblance to what Barney and I saw. What they had seen was an oblong, glowing light with more lights going into it.'

Once the Hills had made the decision to cooperate with John Fuller in writing *The Interrupted Journey*, the story of their abduction, which was published in 1966, Betty's major concern was for her family. She wrote her mother a long letter explaining why they had come to this decision and how they felt it was, in fact, going to ease rather than complicate their situation. What they hoped to do was set the record straight, to tell the story as it really happened, correcting much of the misinformation that had appeared in the press.

Betty Hill opted to share her thoughts, aware of how her mother might react to a rebirth of publicity. Of course, she and Barney received agreement and support from the family. They also had an almost parental attachment to Delsey, their dachshund, who traveled with them most everywhere and was presumably abducted with them.

In fact, Barney Hill, regarded as an intelligent man with a keen wit, could always be counted on to amuse family and close friends with slightly off-center and tongue-in-cheek remarks about his own experience. Once the Hills had adjusted to what they had experienced, he made light of their situation. For example, he once speculated with family members about the problems the aliens must be having deciphering who we are due to the unusual random samples they were taking. He noted the obvious physical differences between himself and Betty, among them their skin color and that he had false teeth.

'Somewhere on their planet,' he would chuckle, 'there is a lengthy scientific report which reads: " On Earth the men are tall, black and have removable teeth. The women are short, white and have their own teeth. And the children ..."' he would pause for effect. '"The children are long, squat and have pointed noses."' He would smile as he made this obvious reference to Delsey, their dog.

Barney Hill would be pleased by the family reaction and offer another speculation. He would recall that the first time the craft had approached them, he had been alone several hundred feet from the car where Betty and Delsey waited. The aliens bided their time and took both of them and the dog a few minutes later. Suppose, joked Hill, the aliens had taken him alone. He suffered from high blood pressure and ulcers, so the fear and anxiety could very well have killed him. What would they have done with the corpse? Possibly eject it out in space. (This was 1961, long before man walked on the moon.)

Hill would continue: 'Suppose the first astronauts were on their way to the moon and what do they pass but a dead black man floating around in space. They'd probably say, "My God, they're everywhere."' His own laughter would be the loudest.

These were the reports of public abductees. Secret abductees do confide in their families in many instances but probably have the same apprehensions about their reactions.

Mrs. K., the secret abductee of Ogden Center, Michigan, could not hide what was happening from her family with any more success than Ellecia Gruen since they, too, shared the anxiety of seeing UFOs fly over their houses for three months and were told of her childhood encounter. Like Mrs. K., her family is convinced that something supernatural or satanic rather than extraterrestrial is occurring and will not discuss their lives at all.

For years, Jessica Rolfe, who remains a secret abductee,

dared not discuss her evening conversations with the *Kuran* even with her mother, father, or older sister. Today, she rarely speaks of her sister, merely intoning, 'We're not alike at all,' and apparently there is no close feeling between them. Her relationship with her mother is something else entirely.

'About two years ago I sat my mother down and told her everything,' Rolfe explains. 'My father had died and I thought she was ready to hear the truth about me. To my surprise, she took it well, wanted to hear as much as I could tell her and even said she had suspected that there was something unusual about me for some time.

'She told me something that slightly stunned me. I am adopted, but I have been able to locate the name and place of birth of my natural mother, even though I have no idea where she is. My parents—that is the Rolfes—adopted me when I was three days old. At the time, the nurse declared that she had a message from the natural mother, who had said, "Tell them she may seem different, but to please love her anyway."'

Admittedly, Rolfe had no concrete idea what her natural mother—who, like her adoptive parents, was Jewish—had in mind when she asked the nurse to relay that message. It had bothered her mother for twenty-five years. Now Rolfe is convinced that somehow her natural mother had, herself, had encounters with alien races or suspected her young daughter would. Of course, it is also entirely possible that the natural mother meant nothing obscure, that there was no hidden meaning. She could have just been pleading with the Rolfes to take good care of her baby in spite of the fact that she was not their natural child.

Rolfe also confided her experiences to her former husband, whom she divorced a few years ago. Though the abduction was not specifically the cause of the divorce, Rolfe does admit 'he felt he was sharing me with my past and was resentful. It became too much for him. Y'know I don't burden everyone with information about the *Kuran*, but it is with me at all times and will be for the remainder of my life. It makes relationships difficult. I have to hold something back.'

## FAMILY LOYALTY

We can also speculate what would have happened if a secret abductee confided in a friend or lover only to find that person skeptically relating the occurrence to other persons. Certainly, even if the abductees are not obsessed with their experience, they insist that they are being less than honest if they hold back something as important to them as their encounters.

Approval is an abstract entity everyone seeks from family, friends, teachers, colleagues, teammates, or whomever. It is not approval for their stories that the abductees seem to want but reassurance from those closest to them that support is given without second thoughts.

Generally speaking, the abductees, both public and secret, who have decided to rely on their families have received the needed support. True, there have been divorces and estrangement, but, overall, kinship has remained strong. No abductee is without at least some close companionship or family tie today. Moreover, none that we are aware of appears to be used by a spouse or lover for their celebrity or curiosity value.

The need to give and receive love and to prove they are still human and have worth has been exhibited in very personal ways. A very odd coincidence occurred to the men in the work crew that witnessed Travis Walton's abduction and to Walton himself. Of the six other men on the crew, two were already married and three married shortly after the incident, as did Walton. All six of the wives conceived within a year and all six men had new sons.

No matter what the consequence of going public, whether it was deliberate or accidental, the abductees have not lost those who were close to them; indeed, they may be appreciated more. For the families, it was not simply a matter of facing the neighbors, of absorbing some ridicule because of the relationship. It was a matter of accepting a share of the pressure from the community, the media, and the government. It has not always been easy, but families do not ask for rewards.

## Chapter Five

# You Read It Where?

The most outspoken of the public abductees have become wary of the press and broadcast media over the course of the years since their experiences became known. Despite their public openness, it is becoming increasingly difficult for reporters to obtain interviews with the abductees because they are either tired of being asked the same questions over and over or have become disgusted with the general handling of their cases. Several of the interviews for this book would not have been possible without the reassurance of researchers who had become friendly with the witnesses.

It is not that the contactees expect front-page headlines or lengthy articles heralding them as the voices of a new age. They all admit that the newspapers have a right to print skeptical remarks. They do, however, resent the descriptions that characterize them as being strange and articles that are written from hearsay evidence after reporters either have been unable to reach abductees or after an interview. Ripoffs and fabricated quotes seem to abound.

Often articles have been published without the consent or knowledge of the abductees. Betty and Barney Hill fit this pattern.

'We didn't want to go public,' Betty Hill told us. 'We had told some family and a few close friends, but it was nobody's business as far as we were concerned. We had never thought about the nation – even the world – finding out.'

## YOU READ IT WHERE?

It began when a reporter from a Boston newspaper, at a cocktail party one evening weeks after the abduction, was casually told about 'this Portsmouth couple' who claimed to have been captured by extraterrestrials.

The reporter contacted the Hills, but they refused to give him an interview, making it quite clear that they had no desire to see their names in print. Following their refusal, the reporter called Dr. Benjamin Simon, the psychiatrist who had conducted the Hills' hypnoses. He demurred, saying it would be improper to discuss his patients and their story.

The reporter eventually hit pay dirt. Several months before, the Hills had reluctantly agreed to speak about their experience with a UFO group in Quincy, Massachusetts, where – unknown to them – they had been secretly tape recorded. To the Hills' shock and dismay, a fragmented and distorted version of their story, lifted from the tapes, appeared in a newspaper and was immediately picked up by the wire services.

On reading the article, the Hills agreed that it was incomplete and made them look ridiculous. They sought legal advice, since they respected freedom of the press, but they felt that their desire to remain private should have been honored. They were told that since no libelous statements were made, there was little they could do about the article under the law.

After due consideration, the Hills decided they had no alternative. In order to correct the erroneous picture of their abduction that was being repeated over and over in the media, they would face the public head on. So began national radio and television speaking engagements, their arrangement with author John G. Fuller to write their story, *The Interrupted Journey*, and eventually Betty Hill's cooperation in turning the book into a made-for-TV movie, 'The UFO Incident,' starring James Earl Jones and Estelle Parsons.

Betty Hill has achieved a certain celebrity status of her own and can frequently be found jetting around the country doing interviews, lectures on the college circuit, or television talk shows. It was not something she sought, however; nor did she engage in this activity while Barney was still alive. UFOs may be one of her 'causes' today, but it took several years for her interest to blossom fully.

'We didn't even tell the neighbors about our capture,' she remembers as she eases into her weathered sofa and coaxes her dachshund, Brandy (Delsey passed away years ago), to sit at her side. 'We told only a few friends, relatives, our minister and Pease Air Force Base which is only a few miles from Portsmouth. It was a personal thing and we wanted it kept private, Barney especially. After we went public and I got around the country and spoke to many people who had seen things, I got drawn into it more. I'm not thankful to the press, though.'

Of course, one can argue successfully that the Boston reporter had a good newsworthy story and was justified in going after it. Although he published the article against the Hills' wishes, his error may have been that he had half the facts and came very close to holding the Hills up to ridicule. Since they were such intelligent, articulate, and feisty people, they did not suffer great emotional harm.

Mona Stafford, who willingly told her story to reporters despite the protestations of Elaine Thomas and Louise Smith, was not happy with the results.

'I've had reporters just come in and announce that they wanted to interview me and expect me to drop everything to sit with them,' she told us. 'I'd say, "Now wait a minute here, if you want me to talk about it I'll be happy to, but at my convenience." They don't even call first for an appointment, just try to use me, take advantage. That's not right.'

Stafford got so annoyed with reporters appearing at her house with no warning that she turned away a newsman from the Danville, Kentucky, *Courier-Journal*. Rather than make the 'grueling' twenty-minute drive again, the reporter decided to write an impersonal feature story about Stafford. She was appalled when she read his article.

She recalls with anger how he humiliated her. 'He went into

Liberty and spoke to a bunch of people who didn't even know me. Apparently he went into the busiest restaurant in town and asked people about me. They were laughing and going on about my eyes.*They were mocking me and at one point the restaurant owner started pretending he was looking for something. The reporter asked him what he was looking for and he said, "I misplaced my eyeballs here somewhere." There were other things like that and that's what the reporter wrote. It was in the paper.'

Such incidents lead abductees to wonder whether going public was opening themselves up not only to ridicule and censure but also to being put in a position of advocacy as well. On many occasions, they have spoken to reporters and told their story, only to find it blended with the doubting words of scientists and astronomers they have never met. The same situation has occurred on television and radio talk shows. On several occasions, they have been asked to retell their stories, only to find themselves on a panel debating UFOs. Their 'opponents' were usually highly educated and articulate scientists and writers, seasoned performers before the camera who try their best to appear brilliant in contrast to the confused abductee, often succeeding.

Such was the case with Charles Hickson when he appeared on 'The Dick Cavett Show' in January 1974. Although not used to the lights of a television studio, Hickson kept his composure and held his own, even employing a bit of down-home wit. At one point, Cavett asked him why he had not turned around and run when he saw the craft. Noting that Parker and he were fishing, Hickson quipped, 'Well, we had a river, a big river on one side and them on the other . . .', scoring points with the audience.

Following a commercial, Cavett interviewed prominent scientists, obvious nonbelievers, who glibly implied that Hickson was not telling the truth. Since the show was on

* Under hypnosis, Stafford said that the aliens had removed and then replaced her eyeballs during her examination on the craft.

national television, the imputation did its damage. Hickson, who was simply trying to relate his experience, was suddenly widely suspect in the public eye.

Explains Hickson with understandable annoyance: 'I'm less than satisfied by the way we've been treated by the press. People come down here to talk to us and then our names show up in embarrassing ways. Do you know they've made two comic books based on our story? I am not flattered to see myself in a comic book.'

Hickson had other problems caused by the press. A reporter dug up the fact that he had filed for bankruptcy some months before the abduction and used this information as background in a story that questioned Hickson's reliability. Supposedly, financial reversals coupled with a UFO incident was proof of the unreliability of Hickson's word. Since Hickson points out he has yet to make any money on the encounter, there seems to be no relation between the two events.

Travis Walton and the foreman of the work crew that witnessed his encounter with the spacecraft have both been targets of attacks by reporters looking for a good story. In Walton's case, banner headlines were used in area newspapers to recount an earlier run-in with the law when he was still a teenager. Walton says he had passed a bad check but made restitution for it. In the community, the incident was over and long forgotten, but it was used to discredit him in news articles.

Michael Rogers, the foreman of the wood-thinning crew, was also the brunt of a reporter's article in a local newspaper. According to Walton, the writer alleged that Rogers was having problems finishing the job they were on, a government contract to thin a section of national parkland, and had therefore persuaded the crew to concoct the whole story in a brash attempt to save himself. The reporter claimed that 'secret sources' had told him that Rogers had underbid in order to get the contract and therefore wanted to get out of it.

As Walton argues in his book *The Walton Experience*, one of the crewmen had only been working two days, and several others were married, with children to support, and would certainly not have risked losing the job, with all the attendant publicity and possible ridicule, just to help Rogers. In addition, says Walton, Rogers was found in default because of the work delays caused by the UFO incident and lost quite a bit of money, hardly what one would expect if he were participating in a fraud.

The writer, who tried to discredit Rogers, presumably had never checked his facts with the U.S. Forest Service or Rogers, according to Walton. Subsequently, the Forest Service gave the reporter and other media representatives information completely clearing Rogers of the ludicrous charges, including the fact that the man who eventually won the right to complete the contract bid even less than Rogers and made a profit.

Walton and the six crewmen who were witness to the capture suffered another painful experience. Several reporters decided privately that the men had seen the NBC movie 'The UFO Incident,' the dramatization of the Hills' abduction, which had been aired several months prior to Walton's encounter. This, they said, was what could happen when television ran such sensational shows; people would stage similar incidents. Walton swears that he never saw the NBC movie. Each of the men on the crew told him the same thing. No, they had not watched the television film. In any event, Walton's capture was substantially different in several material aspects, and had the reporters really done their homework, they would have seen the differences.

From the stories that pit the abductees against the press, the conclusion could be reached that most reporters seek earthly explanations for the abductees' stories. What is less easily comprehensible is how poorly these abductees have been represented by the UFO magazines, the very publications that are written by UFO experts to promote belief in UFOs and extraterrestrial visitations.

Although they are not widely circulated, there are a number of magazines that cater to UFO enthusiasts, with articles ranging from interviews and biographies of abductees to speculative pieces on energy warps and the black holes of outer space. *Flying Saucer Review*, published in England by the British UFO Research Organization, is probably the largest and most generally respected of the twenty magazines that originate with recognized independent UFO research groups around the world.

Four UFO organizations in the United States are among those groups that publish similar magazines. *The APRO Bulletin* (Aerial Phenomena Research Organization, Tucson, Arizona), the *International UFO Reporter* (Center for UFO Studies, Evanston, Illinois), *The MUFON Journal* (Mutual UFO Network, Sequin, Texas), and *The UFO Investigator* (National Investigation Committee on Aerial Phenomena, Kensington, Maryland) have a combined circulation of approximately eight thousand. However, they are purchased only by members of the organizations through subscriptions.

Of the five unaffiliated UFO-oriented magazines that are published monthly for popular sale in the United States, *UFO Report* is the largest, with a circulation of forty thousand.

Since the editors of these magazines are familiar with most of the material on UFO abductions and have often interviewed the witnesses personally, the magazines are a logical place for authors, historians, and others to do basic research.

While some of the magazines are reputable, we discovered that the magazine stories on the abductees that we interviewed were incorrect much of the time. It wasn't that they fabricated evidence; we found inaccuracies or embellishments that were detrimental to the people they were allegedly trying to help: the abductees.

It is difficult to fault the publications for small misrepresentations. Often the interviews they had with the abductees were conducted within weeks or days of the incident or the hypnotic session that revealed the capture after a long interval. In many cases, the abductees were still in shock; as a result, they told their stories in a fragmented fashion. Once they regained their composure and were able to examine rationally and objectively their experiences, many of the abductees recalled more details, frequently enabling them to clarify and elaborate on their stories.

In the time that has elapsed since their experiences, the abductees have acquired a perspective on what happened to them that often causes their stories to vary somewhat from the original versions told to the UFO reporters. Unfortunately, the apparent differences in the way the abductees now remember their captures and the way some magazines have repeated the stories have caused at least one abductee, Jeffrey Greenhaw, to be skeptical about all media coverage of his encounter.

Greenhaw felt that his story was treated in a very damaging manner by *UFO Diary*, one of the smaller magazines, which takes a favorable approach to those who report UFO sightings. 'No one seems to have gotten the story right, not even them,' he says.

Instead of helping by setting Greenhaw's 'story straight,' the magazine made him look like a fanatic searching for UFOs behind every cloud. Greenhaw used a Polaroid camera to take four photographs of what he believes was an alien being. According to *UFO Diary*, he had the camera with him just in case he saw a UFO because he was aware of reported sightings in the area. In fact, they went even further and wrote that he had 'searched the brush for space vehicles.' In other words, he was UFO hunting, and, lo and behold, he found one.

Greenhaw is perplexed about how they came to these conclusions, unless they thought it would make the story more exciting.

'Don't they know that most policemen in rural areas carry cameras?' Greenhaw said to us. 'People you book have to be photographed. When you take someone to jail in a small town you've got to photograph them before you can take them to the county facility.' He adds that the media reports of his sighting have 'twisted it considerably.'

But editors to whom we spoke said that Greenhaw's

explanation had varied over the five years since his encounter and that they had decided to stick to his initial version.

Jeffrey Greenhaw insists he was not UFO chasing. In fact, he was unaware of any reports of UFOs in the vicinity of Falkville, Alabama, until later in the evening, after he had given the story to the local newspaper. He was routinely doing his job, which normally involved the presence of a camera in his car. Greenhaw contends that the misinformation spread in the media has made his readjustment difficult.

If the UFO magazines are often imperfect in their coverage of encounters and newspapers and newsmagazines sparse, there is one publication that not only attempts to give the best possible information to its readers but also has been of help to many of the abductees. That publication is the *National Enquirer*, the weekly Florida-based tabloid newspaper.

Not only does the *National Enquirer* maintain a UFO department with a full-time editor, but it also has helped those who have had sightings or been abducted to find researchers or physicians near their homes in order to receive aid. One thing the abductees would agree on: Individuals who believe they have seen a UFO or have been captured and don't know where to go for help often find a friend in the *National Enquirer*. It has assisted them in meeting a team from APRO or MUFON and has helped find medical assistance. It often offers to buy the new-found abductee's story if he is willing to sell it.

Travis Walton remembers that he was in pretty shaky psychological shape the first several weeks after his abduction. Yet dozens of reporters were clamoring for his story, telephoning his brothers, who were trying to protect him. The APRO investigators suggested that he might solve the problem by granting one detailed interview, to the *National Enquirer*, which would get the story out nationwide. He agreed.

Four *Enquirer* reporters met him at a hotel in Scottsdale, Arizona, interviewed him in a relaxed manner, and even paid for Walton and his brother, who had accompanied him, to stay overnight. The publication also agreed to pay all expenses of Walton's lie-detector tests and hypnosis, under the supervision of three psychiatrists. (Without this financial aid, Walton said, neither he nor APRO could have afforded the services.) All of these sessions were extremely important to him, he said, in helping him to cope with the experience and begin to relax and live a normal life again.

Carl Higdon was also well treated by the weekly tabloid. He recalls, 'The *National Enquirer* paid me $100 per day and all expenses to go see a psychiatrist in Los Angeles. It was so they could do my story and have a basis when they said I was sound mentally. I think that is a good way of doing things.'

Most tabloid newspapers have had a reputation for reporting only on the sensational aspects of the news. Normally, their pages are filled with unspecific celebrity gossip, recipes, astrology charts, and fad diets. They do not have a sturdy reputation for presenting solid facts, however unwarranted this attitude may be. The abductees, on the other hand, say they are quite satisfied with the way they have been treated by the popular tabloid publications. More so, many say, than with the way they have been treated by more 'respected' writers.

Travis Walton was in the middle of writing his own book, telling every detail he could remember of the abduction and its immediate aftermath, when his friends found a version in the bookstores, a paperback written by a freelance writer who had never even spoken to Walton, just rewritten other press accounts. Walton feels strongly that the other book has cut into the sales of his own work and spread misinformation. He emphasizes that he does not deny any writer's freedom to publish but would rather have the story told in his own words.

Betty Hill is so tired of seeing her own work copied verbatim and published under someone else's name that she has become very guarded about what she will show any writers who speak with her. Hill has been doing original research on UFOs since 1972, gathering information about sightings in New England

and traveling to an isolated spot in New Hampshire that she feels she has identified as a frequent UFO 'watering hole.' She has taken many photographs of the vehicles she's seen, had soil samples taken of their landing spots, and has compiled results and speculations. More than once, after allowing reporters to see the test results, she has found her own notes and writings in print word for word but under someone else's byline. She said she had never received any payment and few thank yous. 'I'm no longer so naive and gullible,' she adds.

Carl Higdon had an unpleasant experience with a television film company. Alan Landsburg, producer of the 'In Search of...' documentaries, wanted to use Higdon's encounter as part of a UFO show for the series. Landsburg's assistant promised Higdon $100 a day as an honorarium. Higdon normally earns more than that but agreed to do the show because it sounded like fun. He took five days off without pay.

At the end of the filming, Higdon recalls, 'The woman gave me $100 and asked me to sign a release. She said it would all be taken care of, that I would get a check for the rest of the money. Now they claim that the $100 is all I get because I signed a release, and I have never even seen the show on television. They never contacted us to say when it would be on locally. They didn't even have the courtesy to do that. You figure it out!'

Charles Hickson is so fed up with reading stories about himself that are untrue that he has taken two steps. First, he will not give interviews unless he is paid for them. As he says, 'You're being paid something, why shouldn't I have part of it? I have been reading about myself for five years now. I've just decided that if the national news media wants to write about me, I'm going to make some money on it.'

Second, Hickson has done something considerably stronger: he has begun to file lawsuits. 'People that wrote articles about Calvin [Parker] and me and has hurt my character and his – well, we're going to have a lawsuit of it. And I don't want any more of it. If I give an interview from now on, they'll print what I say and nothing else.'

Some writers, the abductees insist, are obsessed with discrediting UFO witnesses. Betty Hill and Charles Hickson are among many whose stories have been torn to shreds. Hill is philosophical about it. 'Everyone's got his own pet ideas and he's got to throw out all the evidence that doesn't tie in with his theory.'

Indeed, it doesn't take a genius to see the contradictions between the complete texts of Betty and Barney Hill's hypnosis sessions as published in *The Interrupted Journey* and what some writers have claimed they said. Even if one doesn't believe that they were captured, accuracy is easy to come by when discussing their revelations under hypnosis. It is all in print, in John Fuller's book.

Dr. James Harder, UFO researcher at the University of California at Berkeley, feels that people who are obsessed with disproving the existence of UFOs are hiding something themselves.

'If someone is obsessed with it,' Harder reasons, 'I wonder if they don't have first-hand knowledge of either aliens or some government desire to cover up what we [researchers] are finding out. After all, the abductees are hurting no one, they haven't made big money, they haven't been recognized by the leading minds and seats of knowledge in this country. Why go after them, unless you yourself have a motive?'

Despite their detractors, the abductees who have gone public continue to relate their feelings to all questioners. Because they are willing to speak out, they become personalities in the sense that television and radio talk shows invite them to be guests and the press also feels that at least part of its audience is interested in their lives.

Betty Hill has been on nearly every major talk show, some more than once. She has quite an impressive collection of autographs from stars, politicians, and other celebrities who have been on the shows with her. Even Hill's dachshund,

Brandy, seems to be a seasoned veteran of press inquiries. He sits on her lap during interviews, listening quietly, until cameras are brought out.

'So many camera crews come here that my dog recognizes them,' Hill chuckles. 'As soon as they start taking pictures he wants to pose with me. I think he's one of the most photographed dogs in America.'

Between 1975 and 1978, Travis Walton appeared on most of the national talk shows, but demand for his services has slackened considerably in the last year or so, which pleases him. He says, 'I want to put it behind me.' Walton still agrees to do interviews, and he was one of the guests on the pilot show for the television documentary series 'The Unexplained,' in which he and L. J. Lorenzen, director of the Aerial Phenomena Research Organization, told his story to narrator Leonard Nimoy.

In Las Vegas, a town full of those who love the limelight, Louise Smith has inadvertently achieved more notice than one might expect. She was thrilled to be invited to attend the premiere of *Close Encounters of the Third Kind*, the Columbia Pictures film, and was introduced at the party afterward. She is frequently on talk shows in Nevada and nationally, including 'The Tomorrow Show' and 'The Mike Douglas Show.' She has never accepted payment for her appearances. 'They just give me whatever they want to for expenses,' she insists.

The pseudocelebrity status has had some amusing side effects for Betty Hill. Like Samuel Clemens, she has seen many premature announcements of her own death. Unperturbed by the obituaries, she cannot resist telling some of the anecdotes to visitors.

'A reporter from the *Boston Globe* wanted to do an interview with me, so he called the Portsmouth police for my address and phone number,' she recounts laughingly. 'And they said to him, "She died." He thought that was odd. I mean, working for a newspaper he would have heard this. He checked all the obituaries and I wasn't there. So he called information and got my phone number and called me and he said, "You'd better speak to the Police Department; they think you're dead."'

Betty was just about to call the police from her office on the following day when an officer she knew personally walked in on business.

'I said, "Wait a minute, I want you to take a message back to the station,"' she continues, enjoying the retelling of the story herself. 'He looked at me and said, "Oh, my God! I gotta pinch you."' The officer later told her that the police were considering starting an investigation to discover why she and Barney had both died so young. Foul play was suspected.

'I really don't know how these rumours get started,' Hill continues. 'Another time an acquaintance called and asked me if I was all right. I said, "Sure." He was sort of fishing for what he should say so I asked him what was wrong. He told me he had just read in a UFO publication that I had died Labor Day weekend of cancer.'

Undisturbed by the obituary but wanting to startle the editor, Hill put in a call to his home. 'The moment he heard my voice he started to scream,' she says, snickering. 'He said, "I made a terrible mistake." I said "You sure have."' After promising to publish an immediate correction, the editor told her that he had heard the news at a meeting where everyone was talking about how terrible it was that Betty Hill had died.' He had tried to call me to confirm but the operator came on and told him my number was disconnected, which was not true,' remembers Hill. 'So he assumed it was disconnected because I had died.'

If Betty Hill is the only one who reports having problems staying off the obituary page, many of the abductees have had humorous, if not downright spooky, things happen to some of those trying to interview them or research alien sightings. Most attribute the incidents to the extraterrestrials as if there is some telepathy or force linking them.

Dr. Iris Maack, the Georgia psychologist who has spent many years studying the abductees, says their suspicions may not be unfounded. She explains, 'Generally speaking, 75 percent of the time, when somebody begins investigating this, they have an experience.' Maack says she herself has been thrown across the room by unexplained forces. 'What appears to happen is that any type of exposure to the psi energy involved opens their own minds to the psi within them.'

Mona Stafford has had two experiences that appear to confirm Maack's observations. 'Back last February a reporter and cameraman from Channel 13 came here to film me. When they started talking to me the cameraman suddenly said, "Stop a minute." The reporter asked him what was the matter. He said, "I don't believe what's happened here." He had this box on his side [battery pack] attached to the camera by a short wire, no more than three feet long. And he said, "I walked at least six feet away with that plugged into the camera and I can't do that. I don't know if I can go on with this or not."'

Stafford nervously recalled the afternoon. 'Then the two of them talked about other strange things that had happened to them that day and the reporter tried to convince the cameraman that he had unplugged the wire when he walked away. But he kept insisting "No, I didn't unplug it."'

They finally finished the interview in her home and drove Stafford to the scene of the abduction for further questioning. Stafford recalls, 'There was a lot of snow on the ground. And, just as I got the last word out, all the snow melted, and I just sank right out of the picture. It was like something didn't want me to do it.'

Even Dr. R. Leo Sprinkle, the University of Wyoming psychologist, who flew to Liberty, Kentucky, to conduct Stafford's hypnosis, had problems. 'Tornado warnings were out and they almost couldn't get here because of the awful storm,' Stafford remembers as another example of the strange things that happen when she is interviewed. 'Then Dr. Sprinkle got locked in the bathroom before he could put me under hypnosis. It took us quite a while to get him out. I can't remember that door ever getting stuck before.'

Betty Hill also supports Dr. Maack's theory about energy forces affecting interviewers. 'We had a television crew here and they were doing a series of eight programs on UFOs, so we were filming for hours. As the crew was finally getting ready to leave one of them said, "Well, I can't say as I really believe in UFOs." One of the other witnesses who was here for the filming said, jokingly, "I'll hook you up with one." The crew left. Twenty minutes later they called me yelling, "Tell her to unhook us,"' Hill recounts gleefully, watching for the interviewer's reaction.

'The camera crew said they were followed by something for a good fourteen miles. They were at a public phone, in a panic. They were about to part and go their separate ways but they didn't know what to do. We didn't know either but we said, "Go into the restaurant and have a cup of coffee, give it a chance, it'll leave." So they went in, had coffee and then got in their individual cars to go home. The woman who was the director and producer of the program had the UFO follow her right up to her door. And night after night going home she saw UFOs. All the time she lived there she saw them. She finally moved into the city in the hope that they wouldn't be able to find her.'

Whether these odd occurrences, which perplex Dr. Maack and amuse the abductees, are evidence of psychic energy or mere coincidence is open to speculation since no firm evidence exists to support either argument.

As might be expected, the contactees are always curious to see the Hollywood movie versions of abductions, including their own stories, but they give the portrayals indifferent reviews.

Ironically, Mona Stafford's capture occurred right in front of the drive-in theater where she later saw *Close Encounters of the Third Kind*. Because of this coincidence – she laughs – 'I made somebody go with me.'

'I didn't think all that much of the film,' Stafford comments. 'But I could identify with the female lead, since we are both artists.'

Louise Smith says she enjoyed the movie tremendously, in part because she was an honored guest at the Las Vegas premiere, but she still gave it mixed reviews. 'There were parts of the movie that were very real, but I suppose any entertainment has to have a lot of fiction,' she reasons.

Ellecia Gruen was surprised that the *Close Encounters* aliens looked so similar to the ones she remembers standing at her bedside, while Lydia Stalnaker says she 'agreed with the way it was done until the last part. They made the aliens out like they need not be feared. I'm not so sure about that.'

Surprisingly, none of the abductees that we interviewed, other than Betty Hill, could recall having seen 'The UFO Incident,' the NBC-TV movie based on the Hill abduction. Hill, of course, did see it.

'As far as the relationship between Barney and me, which is the only thing the writers contacted me about (Estelle Parsons also visited her to research her portrayal), the movie was quite accurate. But if I were doing the movie, I would have had the aliens more like the aliens we saw on the craft, real clear cut,' she reflects. 'And the first part, in the car with the kids hollering at us, that never happened. I guess they were trying to set some kind of mood in the movie, but I never had an experience like that in all my life. That I would have changed.'

The abductees have a like-dislike relationship with the press and the rest of the media. Surely, they have been infuriated and hurt by what has been published, but at the same time, Carl Higdon, Betty Hill, and most of the others carefully keep scrapbooks of the articles written about them.

While it does not seem to have been a motivating factor in their decisions to go public, articles and the fame or notoriety resulting from media exposure can be pleasing to the human ego, which the abductees, like all of us, have. They must also admit that it is only through the various media that they can spread the information they feel others have the right to know.

## Chapter Six

# Official Cover-up

Some of the abductees decided to go public specifically because they believed that everyone had the right to know if aliens were visiting the earth. Often, as with most of us, they were ignorant of any official government policy on the subject of UFOs, and since they felt they had done nothing for which they should be ashamed, they stepped forward and contacted either an officer of the law or a person in a position of authority. But the local police, federal agencies, air forces, or other government agencies, according to many of the abductees we spoke to, were indifferent.

Jeffrey Greenhaw is terse in his appraisal of the air force and Federal Bureau of Investigation (FBI) personnel with whom he dealt. 'They just didn't have the sense to listen,' he says. 'So, I didn't take the time to explain everything completely.' He was especially infuriated when the air force turned its back on him because he, too, was an officer of the law.

His statement sums up and parallels the reactions of the abductees who took the time to perform what they consider a patriotic duty. In their minds, the government's record in investigating and explaining their encounters has not been satisfactory. For years the powers within the American government and military have either curtly explained UFOs as unusual natural phenomena or a hoax or declined to make any determination.

## OFFICIAL COVER-UP

The origins of an official American inquiry into UFO sightings date back to 1947 and extend to 1969. Under pressure following the sighting of nine UFOs near Mount Rainier, Washington, by businessman Kenneth Arnold in 1947, the air force established Project Sign, an investigative unit that was assigned the task of collecting all information and data on UFO sightings and encounters.

The investigative unit's name was changed to *Project Blue Book* three years later. Operating under the principle that any unidentified aircraft could pose a potential danger to the security of the country, the program was assigned three main functions. It was to try to find an explanation for all reported UFO sightings; to determine whether UFOs did, indeed, represent a security threat to the United States; and to determine if UFOs were examples of an advanced technology that the United States should study and possibly utilize.

More than thirteen thousand sightings were investigated by air force personnel assigned to the program between 1947 and 1969, the year that Project Blue Book was officially terminated by the military. Blue Book staff members were stationed at air force bases around the country so they would be immediately available to interview witnesses and to seek reasonable, earthly explanations for the sightings.

All sightings of UFOs reported to the military came under the jurisdiction of Project Blue Book during its lifetime. Betty and Barney Hill were interviewed by Blue Book officers after they reported their 1961 sighting to Pease Air Force Base in New Hampshire. The vast majority of cases examined by the air force program, simple sightings of bright circular objects in the night sky, were much more mundane than the Hills'.

For example, of the 1,060 sightings reported to the air force in 1966, 255 were identified by Blue Book personnel as planets or other astronomical phenomena; 270 were deemed to be ordinary aircraft; 32 were labeled weather balloons; 109 were explained as satellites; and 94 were called 'other natural phenomena in the sky.' Only 30 cases were deemed to be truly 'unidentified,' while the 270 remaining cases were found to contain insufficient evidence to draw any conclusions.

Unfortunately, the witnesses to the sightings often took exception to being told by *Blue Book* officers that they had merely seen a weather balloon or a reflection on a cloud when they were sure they had seen an extraterrestrial vehicle. Often the result was bad press coverage from the air force's point of view. One of the most stunning examples was the Michigan 'swamp gas' controversy in 1966.

According to United Press International, at least forty persons, including twelve policemen, reported seeing a strange flying object, guarded by four sister ships, land near Ann Arbor on March 21. All the witnesses independently described a similar vision to the air force representatives. In addition to military personnel, the air force brought Dr. J. Allen Hynek, an astronomy professor at Northwestern University and, at the time, chief scientific advisor to Project Blue Book, to the scene. (Hynek is today the director of the Center for UFO Studies at Northwestern.)

Hynek and the air force concluded that the forty witnesses had all seen swamp gas.

The witnesses and many community officials in southern Michigan were not at all satisfied with the air force's investigation and conclusions. The controversy over the 'swamp gas' explanation raged for days. It was carried by all the news wire services and made headlines around the world. *The New York Times* carried detailed coverage of the investigation and debate for five days in a row, including a page-one story on March 25. Congressman Gerald Ford, Republican leader of the House of Representatives at the time, was quoted as being skeptical of the air force's position.

The Michigan case and other similar incidents did nothing to enhance the credibility of *Project Blue Book*. The swamp gas incident represents a milestone of sorts to UFO believers. They feel that the military's attitude toward the phenomenon since that time has been a source of amusement to those Americans who believe in UFOs and has, in fact, helped to increase the ranks of the believers.

Betty Hill laughs at the air force for its explanation of a sighting made near her home in Portsmouth, New Hampshire. As she tells it, 'There were some people living at the beach about fourteen miles away who saw something they said looked like a flying Christmas tree. Well, the UFO investigator had to come up with an explanation. It was right before Christmas and it was a cloudy night. Portsmouth had a big Christmas tree downtown, so the investigator told them the tree must have been reflected on the clouds and that's what they were seeing. I want to know why it only happened that night.'

She theorizes that one of the reasons so few people 'go public' with their sightings is the incredible turnoff they receive from the supposedly responsible agents of our military/security apparatus. 'This was true when the air force was in charge of investigations and it is still true today,' says Hill.

Since the air force closed *Project Blue Book* in 1969, no military or government agency has had official jurisdiction to investigate UFOs. Both the air force and the Central Intelligence Agency (CIA) have denied that they have any interest in continuing to study UFO sightings since, spokesmen claim, 'there is no evidence that UFOs pose any threat to the United States.' However, recently uncovered documents, which will be examined later in this chapter, indicate that there may, indeed, be a program for secretly investigating and covering up UFO incidents.

Betty Hill clearly feels that the government has a cover-up mentality that is actually hindering its own information gathering. She says, 'Let's say a person has a sighting. He tells his friends. If he's friendly with someone in the police department, he may tell the police. But that's as far as it goes. Tell an investigator? Oh, no. There have been enough people who have told investigators to get the picture. You tell an investigator, thinking you're going to give him worthwhile information, and the next thing you know he's telling you what you did *not* see. After this happens to about three people in the community, the word gets around: Don't tell investigators.'

Betty Hill felt that the two air force officers who interviewed her and Barney immediately after the 1961 incident were at best 'indifferent.' Barney, however, found that another officer he spoke with at Pease Air Force Base was very helpful, giving him the confidence to talk about the experience.

Despite complaints by witnesses, the air force, because it was charged with the responsibility of 'explaining' each sighting for security reasons, was more careful in questioning the witnesses than other agencies, such as the FBI and local police, that have been doing the interviews since *Project Blue Book* ended in 1969.

Many abductees who went public in the 1970s have complained about the attitudes of the officials who questioned them.

Mona Stafford, who was questioned by a local FBI agent in Kentucky, felt that while she, Louise Smith, and Elaine Thomas were well treated by the agency, the method of inquiry was inadequate.

'I feel as if there could have been so much more to learn from us,' she told us. 'If they had a different way of questioning, if they'd let us tell everything in our minds about the aliens, they'd learn more.' She believes very strongly that the type and style of questioning limited the information the investigator gathered.

Jeffrey Greenhaw's dissatisfaction extends past mere criticism. He is outspoken in his distaste for the military and police personnel with whom he had contact, blaming them outright for many of his present woes.

'My biggest problem here during that time was the law-enforcement agencies,' Greenhaw remembers. 'They put a lot of pressure on me. They tried to make me retract statements . . .

say it wasn't true. I had to leave Alabama for an indefinite period.'

Apparently, the authorities decided that since he was a respected member of the law-enforcement community himself, people might be more inclined to believe Greenhaw. As police chief of Falkville, Alabama, Greenhaw claims he was entrapped by federal agents when they immediately informed him that others had seen the being he photographed and that a UFO had been tracked to the area by military radar. Greenhaw felt that he had been encouraged by them to tell his story, but now he contends that was not what they wanted at all.

'I was done shitty as hell. I was duped by the government,' he explains with bitterness. 'First of all, they told me they had seen a spacecraft on their radar and had other local reports of sightings of the same alien. I went public thinking I had their support, but they pulled out. I was left holding the bag, looking foolish for saying what I knew was true – that the being I had photographed was not from this Earth.

'If the government had released just one little statement in 1973, other people might have come forward with information that would have saved the day.'

Greenhaw is convinced that much of his subsequent misfortune is a direct result of the government's encouragement of his public stance and later decision not to show the evidence he says it has. He is convinced that his courage in stepping forward led to his downfall. He was forced to resign his job; he was open to ridicule. He says he would not be surprised if 'some of the people that came after me were put up to it.'

'I looked so foolish,' he begins as he enumerates the difficulties he had because he would not recant his explanation of the encounter. 'I've already said that my wife divorced me, couldn't take being with me through all this. I lost my job and my trailer was burned down. They just wanted me out of town. I think it all could have been avoided if the air force or someone had been up front. I know there was a cover-up in my case.'

Greenhaw emphasizes his displeasure with his treatment by American authorities by citing organizations and officials of other countries who have invited him to their nations to speak on his experience. He points out that other countries seem to take the subject more seriously than our government.

Indeed, the Soviet Union has established the UFO Investigation Commission, a subcommittee of the All Union Cosnautics Commission, and the French government has given official sanction to the Centre Nationale d'Études Spatiales. They are just two of the countries that have begun to support UFO research. Greenhaw adds that he has received pamphlets and other material from these centers and finds it most reassuring.

Like Greenhaw, Travis Walton is suspect of the government's involvement in his case, albeit on a much smaller scale. He believes that a Washington writer who has been a chief source of derogatory information published about his case may be on a secret government payroll. Walton's opinion comes from hearsay evidence, so he cannot prove it, but he feels the man (whom he will not name) has gone overboard with attacks on him and the men who witnessed his abduction.

Walton also finds it odd that despite all the national attention his case received and all the media interviews he has done, no one who identified himself as being from any government agency has ever contacted him. He thinks the military or FBI should be curious to get all the details on record by now.

Another UFO witness who believes he is the victim of government harassment has been hiding out in California and using the code name 'David' (presumably because he feels he is up against the government 'Goliath') when contacting UFO organizations.

While in the army a few years ago, 'David' was assigned the job of guarding a crashed vehicle he is positive was a UFO. He claims that the bodies of dead aliens were removed from the craft for examination. 'David' does not give media interviews, but he told both Betty Hill and Aerial Phenomena Research Organization investigator Harry Lebelson in separate conversations that he fears the FBI and the CIA are after him, trying to terrorize him into silence.

Says Betty Hill: 'He didn't spell it out, but you can tell he's afraid he might be found shot in the back one day.'

Lebelson concurs. 'David is very frightened,' he explains. 'He's sure his phone is tapped and won't even give out his number to us.'

Is harassment part of an organized cover up? Most of the witnesses and UFO experts believe that it probably is. Jeffrey Greenhaw says he saw the radar reports and testimony from other witnesses that the government had, which it refused to release in his case. 'I know there was a cover up. For sure!' he states firmly.

'I'll be glad when the government comes out and admits what they know,' exclaims Betty Hill. 'They have crashed UFOs and bodies of dead aliens. If they'd release the reports they'd put an end to all the wild rumors, fears and speculations.'

Dr. James Harder, APRO director of research, points to the media revelation in January 1979 that the CIA has been investigating UFOs for twenty years.

'It took the Freedom of Information Act suits to get classified material, so there must be lots to cover up,' Harder contends. 'It seems to go beyond the need to protect their credibility or to protect earth from enemies. Look at some of the things that have come out. The CIA said it hadn't studied UFOs since 1953, then 2,000 pages pulled out by brute force show that there have been many investigations and studies since then. I wonder how much more there is that we can't get at.'

Jessica Rolfe, who had access to much information on UFOs and government involvement while serving as hostess for a 1975 radio show on extraterrestrials in New England, is convinced beyond doubt that high government officials have concrete evidence that aliens either visit this planet or live in remote corners of the earth.

'Let's say they do know the truth,' Rolfe theorizes. 'Let's

even say that Jimmy Carter and other leaders of the world have encountered aliens themselves, which I think is a possibility. Do you think they would tell us? If they did, they would be risking the order and structure of our societies. They fear that people would no longer have respect for them and their power if they knew that beings of a higher order were reachable. Either they'd flock to the aliens for guidance or chaos would reign. At least that's the scenario I think the government fears.'

Whether Rolfe's theory has any real basis or whether it is just an imaginative speculation, some feel that the government does, in fact, know more than it will admit about UFOs. Indeed, information released in 1978 to GSW, an Arizona-based independent UFO research group, after two Freedom of Information Act lawsuits (and to Citizens Against UFO Secrecy and the National Investigations Committee on Aerial Phenomena after separate lawsuits) seems to indicate that there has been some sort of cover up by government agencies, although no proof of alien or UFO capture can be substantiated.

The documents showed that the CIA has been conducting extensive UFO surveillance since 1949, utilizing its U.S. and embassy facilities around the world, and the most of the research is top secret and available only to the CIA, the National Security Agency, and the White House. In addition, it has become apparent that the air force may be perpetuating a cover up of military sightings.

Air force records collected under the three actions brought by the UFO research groups proved that NORAD (North American Air Defense Command) had been actively observing and recording UFO activities. The files include a 1975 air force memo instructing public information officers to avoid mentioning that there were many sightings near bases for fear that the air force and UFO research might become linked in the mind of the public.

During two weeks in 1975, brightly lighted, fast-moving

vehicles were observed hovering over nuclear weapons storage areas and at at least four air force bases (Loring in Maine, Wurtsmuth in Michigan, Minot in North Dakota, and Malmstrom in Montana). The witnesses to the approach of the circular vehicle included missile launch officers and NORAD commanders who reported that the objects hovered over the nuclear weapons silos on their bases, often coming as close as ten feet from the edifices.

Each time the aircraft were sighted, teams of F-106 interceptor jets were ordered to pursue the unknowns. In every instance, the jets were unable to make contact with the craft.

According to a story that appeared in the *Detroit News*, an air force press spokesman insisted that there was no follow-up investigation done on any of these flights, a statement that is difficult to believe considering that all four were silo bases assigned to the Strategic Air Command.

The CIA papers obtained by GSW added even more puzzling revelations pertaining to the question of a government cover up. For example, the agency had examined thoroughly the story of two Iranian pilots flying American F-4 Phantom jets in that country in 1976. The two pilots pursued a brilliantly luminous object in the sky that ejected a smaller craft that headed straight for one of the Iranian jets at high speed. The Iranians tried to fire at the smaller UFO, but their instruments went dead. At that point, the smaller UFO returned to the mother craft, and the vehicle vanished. This is one of the tales that GSW says were contained in the CIA documents.

One of the CIA documents contained testimony from two retired air force colonels that seems to confirm Betty Hill's conjecture that dead aliens have been captured. The officers reported having seen a crashed UFO in Mexico, near the Texas border, and said that the dead bodies of several aliens were taken to Langley Air Force Base in Virginia. What happened to them after their arrival at Langley remains a mystery.

These revelations infuriate the abductees. It is just the sort of information – however speculative – that can mean the difference between ridicule from neighbors or normalcy in their everyday lives. They feel that if the government has this type of information in classified papers that the public, after Freedom of Information Act suits, can get to see, then there must be more in top secret files. Every piece of information that is released makes the skeptics wonder more about the possible accuracy of what the witnesses have said. Some abductees, for example, Louise Smith, Betty Hill, Carl Higdon, have received letters and telephone calls from people who say they would not believe them if it were not for the released files.

The open files make it easier to believe claims that witnesses such as Jeffrey Greenhaw and 'David' are being harassed into silence by certain federal agencies. The combination of what they have read in the newspapers and what they have seen happen to other abductees leads many witnesses to suspect that a government presence is probable in their case as well.

Dr. Iris Maack, who is involved with UFOs because of her psychological pursuits in helping abductees adjust to the experience afterward, reports that she, too, has been investigated. She is convinced that the American government fears that the aliens are among us or suspects the possibility and is keeping a watchful eye.

'A leading physicist, I can't mention his name,' she explains, 'told me there was a file on me, presumably a government file, in which I was linked with the aliens. In fact, he said they thought I was a liaison from space, or a liaison with the space people.'

According to John G. Fuller in his book *The Ghost of Flight 401*, which chronicled the brutal treatment given four air force officers who saw a UFO by U.S. security personnel, our military/security apparatus has one guiding rule when confronted by UFO reports. That rule seems to be: 'Since we don't know how to defend ourselves against them, it is better to deny their existence than to take the chance of causing a public panic.'

Mona Stafford is the only abductee who finds some degree

of merit with that official position. All the others feel strongly that the public should be informed. But, remembering her own immediate reaction to the capture, Stafford remains more compromising. 'If everyone was like I was,' she reasons, 'we'd kill ourselves. There would be such a panic it would be terrible. Of course, now I understand it. But it took awhile for me to.'

After the multiple UFO sightings in southern Michigan in March 1966, which the air force labeled 'swamp gas,' the public image of that service branch became tarnished. For 20 years there had been all sorts of too-simple explanations by the air force for UFOs seen in the sky, and the government realized the nation had lost faith in official reports. A considerable credibility gap was created after the nationwide press coverage of the 'swamp gas' incident, and Americans everywhere began to doubt the official explanations.

The beginning of the end for *Project Blue Book* actually happened the year before the 'swamp gas' incident. In 1965 nearly two hundred residents of Texas, Oklahoma, Kansas, Nebraska, Colorado, and Wyoming had reported seeing four UFOs in flight formation. The vehicles were easily visible night after night and shined with brilliant colors. Rather than explain this phenomenon in pseudoscientific terms, the *Project Blue Book* officers simply announced that the rather large number of witnesses had all seen four stars in the constellation Orion, millions of miles away, not low-flying, disc-shaped spacecraft.

The citizens of the six states approached their congressmen and senators in search of explanations. The elected officials filed inquiries with the air force.

Shortly thereafter, a similar sighting occurred in northern New Jersey in January 1966. The mayor of Wanaque, four policemen, and hundreds of local residents watched as a brilliant, roundish craft hovered over the area. The air force announced several days later that they had seen a special helicopter. The people were skeptical but quiet until another air force spokesman let it slip to a reporter that there had not been any helicopters in the area that night.

The residents contacted their congressmen and senators requesting a full investigation.

Two months later came the Michigan sightings, witnessed by at least forty people, some of whom would be considered highly reliable by anyone's definition (college professors, students, policemen, etc.). Congressmen Weston Vivian of the local area and Gerald Ford, House minority leader, jumped into the fray, demanding an investigation of the air force handling of these sightings.

The public was seeking answers, not simple excuses. Government agencies had to do something. So they contracted with a professor at the University of Colorado to issue a report that would explain it all.

On October 6, 1966, in an effort to appear sincere in the desire to determine what UFOs might be and if they existed, the Air Force Office of Scientific Research awarded a $313,000 grant to Dr. Edward U. Condon, a professor of physics at the University of Colorado. Condon was to head up a 'totally independent study' of UFOs using duplicates of air force reports to date and any other material deemed necessary to complete the study.

It was, in fact, such an unbiased, independent study that on January 25 1967, barely three months after he had received the contract to conduct an eighteen-month investigation, Condon predicted before a Corning, New York, honorary scientific fraternity what the result would be. According to the Elmira (N.Y.) *Star-Gazette*, Condon told the fraternity members:

> *Unidentified flying objects are not the business of the air force . . . It is my inclination right now to recommend that the government get out of this business. My attitude right now is that there is nothing in it . . . But I'm not supposed to reach a conclusion for another year.*

This was what the taxpayers of America were spending more

than $300,000 for, and the head of the study group already announced his conclusions.

As some of the abductees still insist today, the Condon story goes even deeper into the cover up than the attitude of its director. After the report was completed, a memo surfaced that discredited the Condon Committee in the eyes of many individuals even further. The memo, written by air force project coordinator Robert J. Low to the University of Colorado on August 6, 1966 – two months before the grant was issued – indicated the kind of study the air force was interested in arranging:

*Our study would be conducted almost exclusively by non-believers who ... could and probably would add an impressive body of evidence that there is no reality in the observations. The trick would be, I think, to describe the project so that, to the public, it would appear a totally objective study but, to the scientific community, would present the image of a group of non-believers trying their best to be objective, but having an almost zero expectation of finding a saucer.*

The Condon Committee could not find any reason for the government to continue the study of UFOs. According to a series of articles that appeared in *The New York Times*, of the twenty-five thousand cases available to the committee for study from the records of the air force and other agencies, it chose to examine only ninety. Although the committee of expert nonbelievers could not come up with a reasonable earthly explanation for thirty of the ninety cases (fully one-third), the report concluded that there was nothing unusual about any of the sightings and that the study of UFOs could not be justified.

When one examines the rather lengthy report of the Condon Committee, which few have done precisely because of its length, it is surprising to find that despite the healthy budget the committee had for 'original' research, most of the work it did consisted of reprinting old air force releases and related papers on astronomical, meteorological, and other natural phenomena that were obtained from government agencies at little or no cost.

Several members of the committee also had a good time following up on the more bizarre cases. For example, Dr. Condon became amused with the case of a kook who called himself 'Sir Salvador,' an agent of the 'Third Universe.' Dr. Condon called Washington, in all seriousness, and relayed an offer from the 'Third Universe' through the knightly Salvador to build a spaceport in the United States. If he had only done this, Condon might be forgiven. However, he frequently relayed messages from fringe or kook elements to government officials.

Other subjects that were studied by committee members, who were bent on proving UFOs could not exist, included reviews of human perception problems, optical mirages, cultural mores, the effects of radioactive gases emitted by the sun, the possibilities of hoaxes and conspiracies, and the human desire to be written up in the press. In other words, the Condon Committee seemed to have spent most of its time discrediting the witnesses rather than investigating UFOs.

Herbert Schirmer was a witness whose case is most often remembered. He appeared before the Condon Committee in high spirits, wanting desperately to explain what had happened to him and hear what the government planned to do. Like Jeffrey Greenhaw, Schirmer was a policeman and had been patrolling his beat in Ashland, Nebraska, in December 1967 when he saw a bright flash several yards in front of him. He made a succinct notation in his log: 'Saw a UFO, believe it or not.'

As days passed, the events of that night continued to haunt him, and he realized he could not account for a chunk of time. Schirmer submitted himself to hypnosis, and it was 'discovered' he had been abducted by a metal craft, the shape of a football field with a silverish glow. Inside he was pleasantly interrogated by several humanoids, five feet tall, with gray-white skin, large slanted eyes, and slits for mouths (a description matching that of so many other abductees). The aliens asked him about electric power sources and showed Schirmer how they extracted electricity by connecting their generators to high-voltage wires at a nearby power plant. They ended the encounter by telling Schirmer that they often visited earth, but with no pattern, and would someday in the future reveal themselves publicly.

Schirmer told his story to the Condon Committee. Like so many other witnesses, he was merely dismissed, never receiving any other explanation for what might have happened to him if it was not as he remembered it.

In July 1968, before the Condon report was completed, the U.S. House of Representatives Committee on Science and Astronautics held a symposium on UFOs. Dr. Condon's objectivity was disputed because of his speech in Corning and his telephone calls emphasizing information from fringe elements. Nothing was agreed to at the symposium, but it was decided that the subject should be examined further.

In December 1969, the air force announced the cancellation of *Project Blue Book*. The Defense Department had determined that there was no justification for the program under national security precautions. Thus, the military bowed out, leaving the impression that the government was convinced that UFOs were nonsense.

From that time there have been no overt U.S.-sponsored investigations, yet there must be more interest than the government will openly admit. With all their denials and scoffing, the air force has contracted with Betty Hill to speak at bases in New England and show her photographs and slides of UFOs, many of them taken in southern New Hampshire.

Hill not only shows photographs. She has taken selected officers, those she feels she can trust, to the area outside Portsmouth where she has seen and photographed numerous UFOs. Hill says she is amused at how these officers, who publicly insist they know nothing of UFOs, react when they are treated to flybys of unidentified craft.

'They jump right up and down,' she says, laughing.

Hill further maintains that the air force is still deeply involved in investigating UFOs, but her argument is based on her close friendships with several of the pilots' wives from nearby Pease Air Force Base.

'All the officers' wives are complaining, especially the pilots' wives,' she told us. 'The pilots are out chasing UFOs around here some nights and when the wives ask the husbands about it all they say is "It's top secret, we can't tell you." The wives are furious because the men are never home nights.'

Not one for subtlety, Hill has tried to discuss this with a colonel at Pease, asking in her inimitable manner, 'Why don't you stop harassing UFOs?' She reports the colonel replied, 'We don't make policy, we follow it.'

Since there is no reliable federal agency to which the witnesses can turn today, they must seek out independent UFO organizations. From the abductees' point of view, this is usually a helpful move, yet at the same time the competition between these UFO investigative organizations may be hampering the work they do. Some abductees whisper that these groups are unwittingly helping the government perpetuate precisely the cover up they are so irate about. They are jealous of each other, bicker often, and frequently attempt to discredit anything the other group has that they don't.

Dr. R. Leo Sprinkle, the University of Wyoming psychologist who has been investigating UFOs since 1950, is aware of the problem, although he is not overwhelmingly concerned.

'Sometimes there is a confrontation as to who has a "claim" on a certain witness,' he admits. 'Some investigators have made big money on their work and get national play. The abductee can find himself in a tug of war on occasion.'

Mona Stafford, Louise Smith, and Elaine Thomas got caught in just such a squeeze two months after their abduction in 1976. Although an APRO field investigator was the first UFO researcher to approach them, by the time Dr. Sprinkle could get to Liberty, Kentucky, from the University of Wyoming to conduct the hypnotic sessions, two other UFO groups were on the scene. CUFOS and MUFON both had investigators there and disputed APRO's right to speak with the women. They wanted Dr. Sprinkle to perform the hypnosis as long as he was there but did not want to share the information with APRO, claiming they had squatter rights on the women. Sprinkle normally works for APRO and his trip had been arranged through that organization and the *National Enquirer*, so he would not agree. Finally, after many wasted hours, APRO and CUFOS agreed to a sharing arrangement. By that time, Sprinkle was in a hurry to catch an airplane, and the women, particularly Stafford, had begun to get more nervous than they might otherwise have been. Who knows how much was lost because of this bickering?

At least in Kentucky the sides got together. Travis Walton found himself receiving more flack from the UFO groups he refused to speak with than he did from the press or government. He feels that GSW tried to discredit him after he chose to speak with APRO instead.

As Walton tells it in his book, *The Walton Experience*, William Spaulding, director of GSW, had been in contact with his brother Duane even before Travis's return. Spaulding had promised to help in any way, but when Duane eventually telephoned him seeking a physician to examine his brother, Spaulding did not come through to their satisfaction.

The man he sent the Waltons to see, it turned out, was not an M.D. at all but a former marine corps medic now practicing hypnotherapy. Duane felt that the 'doctor's' office was not up to the standards the Walton family required; therefore, he took Travis out of the office without much delay. Eventually, Travis underwent hypnosis with Drs. Harder and Sprinkle under the auspices of APRO. Then the fun began.

The hypnotherapist, possibly regretting that he had lost such a prize for GSW, began a direct assault. Walton feels that no media remarks were more damaging, both in the public's mind and in his own mind, than those released by the alleged 'doctor.' The hypnotherapist told the press that Walton had fabricated a hoax and was a habitual user of LSD and other drugs. He had obviously been hallucinating. (Both a hoax and a hallucination? How is that possible?) Of course, that did not explain how six people claimed they had witnessed the abduction, but it did not deter the detractors.

Spaulding later made several references to 'holes' in Walton's story and his initial noncooperation with GSW as a sign that there might indeed be a hoax. All these remarks were published by one reporter or another and hurt Walton deeply. The attacks did not shake Walton's story or that of the six witnesses one iota.

While the bickering may seem silly to the scientists involved in the research and to Betty HIll, who just shrugs off the members of the competing UFO research organizations who try to discredit her from time to time, the point is these groups seem to be at loggerheads for no reason. The possessiveness and rivalry among these groups only helps those in the federal agencies who want to forget the whole UFO business. When APRO or MUFON has a witness go public, and a rival group goes out of its way to discredit that person, the result is obvious. The credibility of the abductee is eroded.

The differences help to recall another case. In 1961, only weeks prior to the Hills' abduction, a farmer in Eagle River, Wisconsin, told of giving some cool well water to three tiny men he said came out of a disc-shaped aircraft. In exchange, they gave him four wafers that they had been eating. The farmer ate one, kept one as a souvenir, and gave one to the air force and one to NICAP for study. No report was ever issued by either the military or the supposedly independent NICAP.

What happened to the independent study? After receiving considerable publicity as the holders of the fourth wafer, NICAP suddenly announced that they did not intend to analyze the wafer because of the widespread notoriety. The organization was quoted by United Press International to the effect that it had more important things to investigate and would spend no more time on the Eagle River business. Did NICAP lose interest, or did they just decide not to share whatever information they had?

Chapter Seven

# Suddenly Aware

Establishment scientists, psychologists, psychiatrists, and physicians who have never met the abductees are apt to feel that the encounters they describe are delusions or fantasies of some sort. One of the first things an investigator does when he meets someone who thinks he may have been abducted by a UFO is try to determine if the individual is 'normal' in the everyday sense.

If a psychological problem is diagnosed as the source of the abduction story, it is treated promptly. Psychologists and scientists who interview the witnesses not only want to increase the list of verified abductees but to determine if there are serious physical or mental disorders.

All of the abductees interviewed in this book have been 'verified' by experienced UFO researchers. Each has been questioned, some under hypnosis, and had a psychological profile prepared by at least one of the trained professionals. In truth, these researchers are not necessarily completely convinced that extra-terrestrials are visiting earth, but they are in total agreement when they say that these people have had a 'valid experience' and are not suffering from some form of delusion or fantasy.

These researchers have devoted many years to the study of UFOs, abductees, and the aftereffects of contact with aliens. Dr. R. Leo Sprinkle, psychologist and director of counseling services at the University of Wyoming, is the author of numerous articles on the psychological and psychic implications in the investigation of UFO reports.

Dr. James A. Harder, though a professor of engineering at the University of California at Berkeley, has been involved in UFO research for two decades and is a trained, experienced hypnotist. As director of research for APRO, he has studied hundreds of case histories.

Psychologist Dr. Iris Maack trained at Duke University, where she specialized in handling paranormal patients. She has personally studied and/or counseled fifty abductees.

The fact is, no matter what the researchers' personal attitudes may be, they have not been able to dismiss the stories of the abductees with any accepted psychological technique. The only 'treatment' the abductees appear to need is counseling. Once they have accepted the notion that the only explanation their conscious and subconscious minds can recall for the unaccounted loss of time or unusual recollections is that they were contacted or captured by extraterrestrial visitors, the abductees face a difficult period of adjustment.

Their situation must be dealt with on two levels. First, the trauma of being abducted often has a profound effect on the individual's mental health. Second, if the abductees decide to tell family and friends or 'go public,' they must be prepared for unique challenges in social adjustment.

Most of the abductees faced a period of emotional stress as a result of the encounters. They experienced much anxiety because of the missing segments in their stories; later, once the details of the abduction were remembered under hypnosis or intensive questioning, they would recall the terror they felt at the moment of capture. The effect on their health was one of acute stress.

They sought help initially because they could remember seeing a craft but had no memory of what transpired for many minutes or hours thereafter. The Hills, in fact, were so upset by the time lapse and their terrifying nightmares that their health began to decline. Barney's ulcers and high blood pressure worsened, making it impossible for him to go to work, and Betty had several attacks of pneumonia before deciding that they must seek psychiatric help.

Mrs. K., the secret abductee of Ogden Center, Michigan, has been described by psychologist Dr. Iris Maack as irrational on the subject of UFOs, trying desperately to erase all images of her encounters from her mind.

Mona Stafford sought the help of her family physician a few days after the incident, eventually turning to APRO and Dr. Sprinkle for assistance. In fact, Dr. Sprinkle reports that during the first months after they remembered the abduction, Stafford, Louise Smith, and Elaine Thomas would often telephone him in Wyoming, weeping and upset. They expressed their worries about the nightmares they were having and recurrent fears of subsequent abductions. Dr. Sprinkle feels, however, that their psychological profiles were always strong, solid enough so that the women did not have what is commonly referred to as a 'nervous breakdown' from the strains of coping with the experience and community reaction to them.

One abductee, who prefers to remain 'secret' to protect his present employment, suffered prolonged hysteria. This man was too unnerved immediately after the encounter to be hypnotized and has spent much of the last few years 'on the run' from his former home in order to escape being reminded of the memories. His condition has now stabilized, and he says he is working again.

The psychological ramifications of suddenly having to cope with the fears and shock of capture may be about as much of an emotional stress as a human spirit can endure. Add to that the subsequent strains community reaction may place on the abductee and it is understandable how a nervous reaction might result. None of the abductees who have gone public have been hospitalized for emotional problems. Lydia Stalnakar did seek the aid of a mental health clinic because she did not know where else to turn, but she felt that they lacked understanding and training for her situation, so she turned to hypnosis.

For the most part, the abductees have come through the initial months with their psychological health reasonably intact. Friends were lost and new directions had to be established, but all have survived. For some, such as Louise Smith, who moved to Las Vegas, and Mona Stafford, who briefly tried life in Florida, a change of scenery – at least temporarily – was helpful in coping.

Jeffrey Greenhaw has not fared as well, but this is understandable; his story is not a happy one. He sits in his parents' home today, partially disabled from a back injury, his appearance slightly changed to avoid recognition. Greenhaw speaks with bitterness of his country and neighbors. An observer might say that he feels persecuted as he reiterates the hell he has been through. Since Greenhaw has not been in touch with psychologists, researchers can only say that his view of the world and his life is a negative one and his spirits are low.

'I usually don't even like to get into talking about the story, 'cause it upsets me terribly,' he told us. 'I think you can understand why. You can try to forget if you're in my position and maybe that would be healthy, but it isn't really possible. Not when you did your duty and your life changed forever. Yes, I feel that people tried to do me in and, yes, I feel anger today. It has become a hard thing to live with and it may never go away.'

Of course, there is an obvious difficulty in attempting to elaborate on the psychological profiles of the abductees. Since none of them were seeing a psychiatrist or psychologist before the abductions, there is no way of making a comparison with their earlier attitudes. But it suffices to say that their families and neighbors considered them rational people, and according to researchers who have worked with them, they are all healthy, clear-thinking individuals now.

The available medical and psychological reports on the

abductees do lead us to the most fantastic and unexplainable aspects of the experience.

The vision the contactees all recalled has had ramifications that cannot be explained by modern science, for once again, like the UFOs themselves, the next phase of the abductees' stories takes us out of the realm of current accepted knowledge and explanation and into the corridors of parapsychology, psychic phenomena, and unusual medical problems.

Once more it presents a question of whether an outsider can believe what he is hearing, but now the evidence is all too real. For example, according to Carl Higdon, his medical records seem to defy explanation within the confines of modern medical knowledge and practice. Before this abduction, Higdon suffered from recurring uric acid gout and had scars on his lungs from tuberculosis. After the encounter, his blood was tested and found to be 'very rich' by a physician. Higdon has not suffered an attack of gout since the abduction, leading his physician to feel that the problem has cleared up. In addition, chest x-rays taken at the hospital after Higdon's abduction indicated that he no longer has any scars on his lungs.

'I have been told it is unheard of for tuberculosis spots to disappear,' Higdon told us. 'But my lungs are back to normal, there are no scars, no x-ray can find a trace of damage. My doctor doesn't understand it, he shrugs and says to be thankful.

'As to my gout, I'm even more thankful to whatever power cleared that up. With uric acid gout you get kidney stones bad and the pain is the worst thing known to man. In November 1970 I had nine of them, passed nine stones in 30 days. And I'd get two or three every two or three months. And now I haven't had any since the abduction, not since 1974. I would like for some of these ol' boys who don't believe me to tell me why that is. How come my scars and gout are gone?'

More perplexing than Higdon's recovery are the number of abductees who have become psychic or psychically aware following their encounters. There are cases of abductees becoming precognitive, becoming faith healers, becoming clairvoyant, developing clairaudience powers, and displaying virtually every other form of identified psi phenomena.

No one can say for sure what causes psi awareness or extrasensory perception, as it is sometimes called. What is more problematic is that these phenomena do not lend themselves easily to laboratory experimentation, although the Foundation for Research on the Nature of Man at Duke University conducts ongoing studies of the matter.

Researchers cannot even say for sure why psi awareness appears in one case and not in others. Some scientific studies show that this phenomenon results from overactivation of the automatic nervous system or an increase of electric synapses in the nerves of the brain. In ancient times, mystical tradition held that the pineal gland, a cone-shaped gland in the human brain, was the center of the mind or the seat of the soul, and when something 'snapped' in this part of the body, the result would be the birth of psi awareness in the person.

Dr. Iris Maack, the psychologist who has studied abductees, has long been interested in psi awareness but can offer no definitive explanation for what causes the phenomenon, suggesting instead, 'I don't question where it comes from, I just know we have it. Physicists have told me it comes from electrical synapses of the brain. Perhaps this is so. The amazing thing is that a large portion of the abductees, most of whom were not interested in such aspects of brain power, have found that they have become aware following their encounters. This is not just a random handful. I'm talking about a significant group of people. Something in the abduction has turned on a greater level of brain potential in them. And I'm talking about verified cases, people who have passed my scrutiny or that of others. Psi awareness is a reality and psi awareness among abductees is very common.'

If it is difficult to define, harness, and prove psi awareness beyond a reasonable doubt, it is impossible to explain why so many abductees have become psychic. Perhaps it is caused by the stress and trauma of the experience; Dr. Maack insists that 'stress can be the agent in psi awareness.'

## SUDDENLY AWARE

Others might say that the telepathic communication by the aliens triggers further psi awareness or that psi powers are a gift from them.

Whatever the reasoning and whatever one's willingness to accept psi awareness as a reality, the case histories of the psychic abductees are for many of the investigators perhaps the most exciting aspect of UFO research.

Ellecia Gruen's story is the one most fascinating. As she recalls, her encounters began at the age of seven when the aliens appeared at her bedside and gave her a physical examination with scanners. It was not until twenty years later that this incident came back to her conscious memory. Although she was curious about the images flashing through her head, Gruen went about the business of raising a son and caring for a home and a husband. They have a second son now. To this day, Dr. Maack has never had any reason to doubt that Gruen was in fine mental and physical health when the memory returned.

Then, in the spring of 1976, she watched the dozens of UFOs flying over her house in Ogden Center, Michigan. They came by day and by night, making her constantly nervous and causing her two German shepherds to hide in remote corners of the house. It was a time, she admits now, 'when I was afraid to go outside. The only time in my life when I didn't do diddley.'

After a few days of uninterrupted terror, her appliances began turning themselves on and off, suggesting the presence of a poltergeist, a word that comes from the German for 'noisy spirits' that is used to denote unexplained noises and uncontrollable physical disturbances within one's vicinity. Dr. Maack explained: 'Poltergeist is random psychokinesis (movement caused by psychic powers). It is internal, from forces within us such as stress.' In this case, the source could have been Gruen's own fright or that of another member of her household.

By itself, a poltergeist could make even the most rational

among us leave our homes, but Gruen's experience did not stop there. Her hands began to write automatically, in a disassociated state without muscular effort or mental direction on her part. She would find after these uncontrolled sessions that she would have reams of poetry in front of her written in a handwriting other than her own.

As the spacecraft continued to circle her home, her family was affected as well. Gruen's one and a half-year-old son uttered three words in a strange language over and over again. Gruen wrote them down, and they were later explained by a language teacher as possibly being Ancient Greek, although no one has been able to translate the words. Her garden grew within days and with surprising results; a bed of irises reached six and seven feet tall, with convoluted shapes and a generally eerie look to them.

After she had lost weight from the burden of coping with these events and had become depressed and astigmatic, Gruen went outside and confronted the spacecraft, telling them to 'get out of my sky space.' The craft did not return, but Gruen discovered that the poltergeist and automatic writing were only the beginning of her psi awareness.

She found she could 'smell in the future,' sensing when her infant son's diapers had to be changed even before he had soiled them. Future events would appear as a vision in front of her eyes. She found she had the ability to take pain away from herself and others. When her family or friends went to the dentist, she was able to concentrate and convince them that there would be no pain, perhaps a form of unorthodox healing at a distance. She also may have been responsible for the disappearance of a friend's chronic migraine headaches.

These psi abilities and a recurrent nightmare of UFOs prompted Gruen to try to contact someone who might know more about UFO encounters. Eventually, an acquaintance put her in touch with Dr. Harder at the University of California at Berkeley, and through him she was introduced to Dr. Maack, who says that Gruen's rate of accuracy in predicting events has been better than 95 percent in the three years they have worked together. Maack has pictures of unusual footprints in the snow outside the Gruen home, of the odd irises, and of UFOs flying over the fields surrounding the tiny hamlet of Ogden Center.

'I have given Ellecia psi lessons to work with,' Dr. Maack told us. 'These include exercises like "running the cards," in which a regular playing card is placed backside in front of the subject and he or she is asked to determine which card it is, and "remote viewing," in which a photo of a scene, anything from a park to a house, is placed inside an envelope, and the subject must determine what the picture is and something else about it (for example, if they've been there).

'It isn't enough to be aware, you need to work at it, learn your lessons. I have trained her in several techniques, including seeing colors with her hands, precognitive lessons and others. She is a dynamite lady with great abilities. I think doubters who spend time with her would be convinced about the reality of psi.'

Her record of psi accomplishment is outstanding, according to Dr. Maack. In 1978, Gruen predicted that Pope John Paul I would be chosen and then die a month after his election. The previous year she had predicted the second major New York City blackout and also said that looting would take place. Her precognition, that is, the random perception of future events, and her clairvoyance, the extrasensory perception of objects and objective events, have rivaled many of the more renowned clairvoyants.

Gruen can offer no explanation for why these abilities have come to her and does not outwardly credit alien intervention or the stress she experienced. Understandably, she has elected to use the powers for the benefit of her family and friends.

'I'm like a child learning, and every time I learn one lesson I go on to another,' says Gruen, a strong, no-nonsense woman. 'I can control my abilities to predict the future, but not my visions. They come when they want to. The other readings I can control. I can smell with all parts of my body. Some people don't want to believe this, but there is nothing more I can say to them.

'Psi abilities give you a good feeling and sometimes frighten you, although I'm not really afraid of anyone or anything. I know my own future is a straight path and I can tell certain things about other people's doings. If you come to my house I'm not going to look in a crystal ball or that nonsense, but if you're willing and I can sense something I'll speak up if I know you can take it. I think I'm being helpful in that way and I do derive pleasure from my powers, if you want to call them that.'

Another abductee who has developed remarkable psychic powers since her incident is Lydia Stalnaker. She first realized that she had some psychic ability between the time of her second abduction outside Jacksonville, Florida, in August 1974 and the hypnotic session she underwent in May of the following year. She says that under hypnosis she recalled that she was told by the aliens who abducted her that she was 'chosen' for her 'chemistry.' She contends that her abilities were given to her in some way by the aliens, whom she identified as angels of God.

After the second abduction, when still plagued by a lagging memory about what had occurred, Stalnaker began seeing visions of strange humanoid creatures in her dreams. They communicated with her telepathically. These 'voices,' as she calls them, told her to take karate lessons and to improve her nutrition.

'Evidently they didn't think I was physically fit,' she told us. 'I was the lazy type. It was odd for me to feel so compelled to do anything. But here I was going down to take karate lessons, doing exercises, watching what I was putting into my mouth. And I couldn't figure it out. I was not just electing to do what these voices told me, there was no way I couldn't do them. I was drawn to go where they told me to go, eat what they told me to eat. As I look back, I think they were preparing me for the purpose of their choice.'

As days passed, she said that she could tell seconds before that her telephone would ring and who was calling. She developed X-ray vision, the ability to see through solid objects.

The dreams continued, she said, and she was seeing clear visions of aliens sticking needles in her side while she was on an operating table. Eventually, she would come to learn under hypnosis that this was a key point in her story. At the time, it made her worry that something had gone haywire in her system. She agreed to try hypnosis with Dr. Arthur Winkler, an Arizona hypnotherapist. According to Stalnaker and her neighbor, Jerri Betz, during the first hypnotic session, a holly tree that was outside her house broke in half and rolled up a hill toward the building, all on a calm, windless day. Soon after the incident, Stalnaker realized she had 'the gift of healing' and took the tree's movement as a sign from God.

'I had not gone to church for a long time and I guess I had never taken it too seriously even though we were members of the Church of God,' Stalnaker insists. 'I couldn't preach and I didn't know the Bible that well, but the local churches wanted me to become another Katherine Kuhlman (the late nationally acclaimed faith healer and psychic). They wanted me to preach and heal, but I balked.

'I couldn't hold back, though. I would pray and lay hands and disease would go away. I have helped paralyzed people get up and walk. I have witnesses to this and other healings.'

Dr. Harder supports her claims. He confirms that besides faith healing, Stalnaker has performed paranormal diagnosis, the act of determining psychically that a disease exists without the aid of medical science. In fact, her psi abilities have become so impressive that Stalnaker was selected to be one of the guest speakers at the International Parapsychology Conference in San Juan, Puerto Rico, May 28, 1979.

Stalnaker has been 'healing' people diagnosed as having very serious ailments. There are those who believe that in the art of so-called 'faith healing,' the person being healed has his or her faith in himself amplified. In the frenzy of prayer revival meetings, these 'healings' have been witnessed by others in the audience. Few seem to understand the power of the body to 'heal thyself.'

Still, one wonders how Stalnaker obtained the power to instill the belief in self-healing. She was never one to scorn the medical profession. She is a woman who had lapsed in her own religious beliefs, and was not very well versed in the Scriptures, yet she now has developed a following far from her home. Her own self-image has increased because of the abduction and the subsequent psi awareness. If there is the power within us for self-healing, then Stalnaker certainly appears to have the power to induce this phenomenon.

Among other senses she has developed is her ability to 'sense' when a UFO will be in the vicinity of Jacksonville. She claims that when she has the feeling that a UFO is nearby, she often goes to one of the beaches along the Atlantic Ocean and invariably sees one or more craft appear from under the water. (Stalnaker, Carl Higdon, and Jessica Rolfe all claim that the aliens told them they have a base under the water off the coast of Florida, and these claims were made independently of each other.)

'People bug me all the time about showing them a UFO or whatever,' she says. 'On many occasions I have said, "All right, let's go to the beach." I've gone with friends and skeptics and we've always seen something like I said we would. We stand there and the UFOs rise from the water, they pop out, looking like balls of fire.' A neighbor and close friend, Jerri Betz, said she has been with Stalnaker when the UFOs appeared on cue and has no doubts about Lydia's abilities.

Carl Higdon also says he has a 'feeling when a UFO will be near.' He claims that several times his children have bothered him to show them a UFO, and off the top of his head – not premeditated – he has mentioned a certain hour when they should be outside looking in a particular direction. On each occasion, he and his children say a UFO has appeared.

'I can tell when the aliens are around,' Higdon told us. 'Just recently I told the children to go outside at 9:15 P.M. and they'd see something. Sure enough they did. They saw a white light come across the sky. Not blinking, just like a star. And we know it was no airplane. No airplane looks like this.'

Other abductees appear to have developed some form of extrasensory perception as well.

Louise Smith claims she has a 'sense' when her friends and coabductees, Mona Stafford and Elaine Thomas, are in trouble or need to speak with her. On the day Thomas died, Smith says she was unaware of her illness and already living in Las Vegas. Yet she reports 'feeling so low that day, like I was expecting something bad to happen, but I couldn't put my finger on it.'

Mona Stafford has also experienced some psi abilities. She recalls two instances where she had precognition of the imminent deaths of loved ones. When she was staying with her parents shortly after the abduction, Stafford began having a recurring dream in which she saw her mother as a ghost, able to pass through walls, looking 'as if she were dead.'

'In the vision, Mom would always be wearing the green bathrobe I had given her for Christmas,' she recalls, still overwhelmed by the incident. 'So I knew it was her. And for two or three weeks every time I'd see her actually put on the robe it would tear me to pieces. It was as if I knew something, but I couldn't put it into words. It was so upsetting. I just wanted to tell her to take that robe out and burn it.'

A few weeks later, Stafford's mother learned she had terminal cancer.

Shortly after her mother's death, Stafford had a similar precognitive experience with her fiancé. 'I dreamed that he was going to die in a traffic accident,' she remembers. 'And a few weeks later he died exactly as I had dreamed it.'

Stafford has attempted other psychic experiences, but her success has been limited. She says she has 'flown', or moved across a room with her feet off the ground and no mechanical aids, but has not been able to repeat the effort for verification.

She also tells a story she contends to be true about Elaine

Thomas's last days. Stafford believes her friend was communicating telepathically with the aliens but, more specifically, that she was having astral projections, commonly called out-of-the-body experiences.

'Elaine told me about things that happened to her while she was in the hospital before she died,' Stafford told us in the kitchen of her Dunnville home. 'There was another patient in her hospital room. One night strange lights came on in the room, rolling around on the floor and on the walls. The other patient was scared, but Elaine told her to calm down, that it was the UFO "people."

'It was strange in other ways,' Stafford continued. 'Elaine had a ring, a turquoise set in pure silver. She had taken it off when she was X-rayed, but it was on her finger when the strange lights had come into the room. After the lights stopped she realized that the silver had turned black, and the nurse didn't see how it could be from the medication or anything like that. And her finger was all puffy, like there was something with that ring. A connection with the lights, the UFO people and that ring.'

About the same time Thomas told Stafford about her astral projections. She did not confide details about specific incidents but did say, 'I'm going to be gone in a little while and everyone is going to think I'm dead, but I'm not going to be.' Days later she died, but Stafford still insists Thomas is not dead but that her soul is out of the body and the flesh has been destroyed.

Perhaps someone on the scene at the time could have explained the lights flashing in Thomas's room and the tarnishing of her ring. Perhaps her last words to Stafford were not to be taken too seriously, considering the severity of Thomas's illness and the amount of medication she may have been consuming. Yet Stafford has never been sure of the cause of Thomas's death. Doctors listed it as heart failure.

Jessica Rolfe also claims she has been out of the body, what she prefers to call soul projections. She even fears that someday during one of these projections her body will be destroyed and she will be presumed dead.

Like Gruen and Stalnaker, Rolfe has also experienced the internal energy commonly called a poltergeist, explaining that when she loses her temper, objects will inexplicably move around the room or are thrown by an unseen force. Rolfe asserts that she has precognitive powers and the ability to speak telepathically with alien races. The extent of her experiences is not known because she remains silent on much of her psi awareness. She admits her psi awareness and telepathic communications give her a reason to feel superior to the average mortal human being, but she does not flaunt this feeling. Instead, she prefers to keep her talents to herself.

'I think we should understand that we all have or possess a more subtle body,' Rolfe told us. 'It is not the body we inhabit after death, it is the soul. When we use the first person singular pronoun "I," we are really referring to our soul, because that's who we are. The rest is just our flesh. The *Kuran* have told me that there used to be a race on Venus, but that they evolved out of their flesh, I guess to a higher level of being. Flesh and life are not the same thing.

'I mean, I have been able to leave my flesh, my soul has traveled elsewhere in my lifetime. I enjoy these soul projections too much and I'm always afraid I won't come back. I am convinced the *Kuran* or other alien races are the catalysts for the new-found psi awareness many abductees find they have contracted. They speak to us telepathically and in doing so open up lost abilities in our brain that we all have. I think we would all agree or concede that the potential for psi is there in all of us. We all get psychic feelings every now and then because that very possibility is within us. Perhaps unintentionally the encounter experience can unlock that ability.'

This telepathic communication does seem to be the key. Many abductees – Stalnaker and Rolfe, for example – believe that the aliens either communicated fully telepathically or with a mixture of language and mental communication. This could be the introduction to psi awareness. Ellecia Gruen reminds us that she has grown tremendously by continuing discussion with Dr. Maack. Perhaps each abductee has awareness that is not being tapped. Even the 'sense' that Higdon and Stalnaker have when the craft are soon to be in their vicinity could be from some sort of telepathic communication, with the aliens sending greetings in their own way.

'I think we need to understand that telepathy may put us in a more highly evolved category of beings,' Jessica Rolfe adds. 'When a race communicates with a minimum of spoken language they are harmonic and at one with themselves. After all, according to the story of "Mu," human digressions and devolution are directly connected with our construction and creation of languages. Our digression cycle may be over now. Maybe we're moving back upwards on the evolutionary plane and the aliens can sense that.

'As to telepathic communication, I have been out in the fields watching UFOs with other people and each time I seem to be the one who is contacted by the alien races, if anyone is. One time it was because I was wearing yellow and that fascinated them, but more often it was because I made an effort to telepathically communicate my message to them, a simple greeting. They are sensitive to our thoughts, to dogs barking and other sounds. I believe that because they instilled upon me the ability to communicate telepathically, I have since learned other psi lessons. The problem is to control them.'

It is conceivable that each abductee or contactee has developed some psi awareness, but not all have chosen to work at it. Betty Hill, for example, also mentions some psi perceptions but has not worked on them or sought to study with professionals such as Dr. Maack.

'You have to do something with it,' Ellecia Gruen contends. 'I can look at somebody and do what is considered a reading, a clairvoyant study, but that took time and effort to learn. One of my latest abilities to surface is psychometry, which is when you can pick up an object, touch it and be able to tell its history. No psi powers can really happen overnight.

'Now take my eldest son. When all this happened he was

also able to make predictions. It bothered him. The entire experience with the UFOs really shook him. His grades fell and all. So he has just put it in the back of his mind and wants no part of it. I want him to take lessons, to work at it, but he won't. I do think, though, that the fact that he has had some confirmed awareness shows that there is some connection with the aliens or the UFOs or the stress we experienced. In 1976 he went through everything I did and there has been a similarity in results.'

The debate about psychic awareness has been with us for quite some time, with no conclusions. For example, the writings of Edgar Cayce, the barely educated man who was able to heal people by slipping into a trance and prescribing cures, have been a source of fascination for several decades. Few people have really taken this sort of thing seriously. We may toy with the idea of extrasensory perception, but that is usually as far as we allow ourselves to venture.

If it is true that somehow the alien races instill psi awareness in selected individuals, we must wonder how they decide who will be chosen. Of course, there are no answers. If we accept the premise that psi awareness may be self-induced by stress, trauma, or desire, then perhaps we should ask ourselves if these powers are worthwhile, if somehow they can be beneficial to humankind.

Dr. Maack is convinced that the awareness can be beneficial. Whether as a gift or an accident, she thinks we should celebrate our psychically aware citizens and tap the abilities they have for our own betterment. She recalls that for generations government officials have called on 'psychics' for aid when all else failed. Most recently, some police departments have used precognitive individuals to help determine the location of kidnap victims. While not perfect, the accuracy of these psychic deputies has been surprisingly high.

'If we can reach the abductees and tell them whether they have become psychically aware, we could have a group of fantastic psi people,' Dr. Maack believes. 'They would be a super force, not for military or negative purposes, but to explore the powers of the brain and the world to a greater extent.

'It is my philosophy that we are born with all knowledge, or the potential for all knowledge. The brain is like a wonderful computer, the center of the knowledge, a knowledge bank. Psi awareness is practically always a good thing; it's not witchcraft. Think of all the good things these people could do for us – in medical diagnosis, in testing danger zones, in locating missing people or objects, in discovering the extent of human knowledge. If the awareness is a gift from the aliens, I'm thankful for it, but I'm not sure it is. All I know is that it is time we stopped closing our minds to this phenomenon, because it does exist and it has always existed. What are we afraid of?'

One of the medical and biological ironies of our lives is that we cannot fully understand the brain, the organ that gives us the ability for understanding. The thought process can be charted, but it is a miraculous wonder of life that this process is actually quite spiritual. We don't choose to think, we are born with the need to think. If we acknowledge these premises, it is logical that one does not choose to be psychic; it happens.

Abductees, when discussing their experiences, defy skeptics to give them a conclusive explanation for what happened to them if they were not actually seized by an extraterrestrial craft. In the same vein, Ellecia Gruen asks skeptics how she is able to predict future events, to decipher colors and smells with body parts besides her eyes and nose.

And if psi awareness is a gift from the aliens, to what purpose? Are the aware abductees forerunners of a time when the aliens will land and aim to help us evolve to a higher plane? Is it true, as Jessica Rolfe contends, that the aliens have visited us before but that these efforts to help us have been misconstrued? Could this be still another of their attempts?

Scientists have been trying to explain psi phenomena for generations. Christian missionaries have been confronted with witch doctors and voodoo practitioners and unusual cultural traditions and felt compelled to destroy or discredit the people and their ability because it seemed to go against the divine truth of God.

Emmanuel Swedenborg, scientist and philosopher, wrote a book about his alleged travels to other planets, but it was never taken seriously in the intellectual community. Scientists and researchers have neglected psi, either finding it part of the occult or fearing ridicule if they embraced it as a reality.

The psi abilities of Ellecia Gruen, the faith healing of Lydia Stalnaker, the not fully tapped awareness of Jessica Rolfe, all of these powers do not appear to be imagined. They are more of an extraordinary interaction of a person with the greater universe. Overall, the psi awareness is just another facet of the direct encounters since the evidence is there for those who wish to accept it and not substantial enough for those who wish to doubt. The abductees are leaving the question of belief still to be answered subjectively.

## Chapter Eight

# Heavenly Messenger

A major difference of opinion exists among the abductees on the question of who the extraterrestrials are, where they come from, and what it is they want from the planet Earth and its inhabitants.

None of the abductees we interviewed deny the existence of a supreme being as creator of the universe. More important, not one of the abductees has declared the aliens to be outside of God's creation as we know it. Jessica Rolfe, who has lapsed in her Jewish upbringing and considers herself an agnostic, insists that 'the *Kuran* and the other alien races also speak of there being one God that created all the universe. They know that He exists and is a mystery to them in many ways. Unlike us, they just don't believe He intercedes in the day-to-day evolution of the worlds He has created.'

Such statements might spark debate among the limited number of contactees. Most shun a definite position on the origins of the aliens, merely assuming that they are from other planets. It is logical to many of them that the idea of humanoids on other planets does not preclude a God but shows more fully His omnipotence.

At least two of the public abductees are not sure whether the alien races live on other planets. Like others who follow the UFO controversy, they have become convinced they can make a strong case that the aliens are unquestionably 'from God' or 'angels of God.'

## HEAVENLY MESSENGER

The last conclusion is the opinion of Mona Stafford and Lydia Stalnaker. Stafford has described the alien she saw during her second encounter as looking 'the way they were described in the Bible. He had this robe-like thing over him. It just shined. He looked like the sun was shining on him. The clothes were real bright, brighter than any material we have. His hair and everything just glowed.'

Stalnaker has always insisted that she was abducted by angels of God and that her abductors told her that is who they were. Like Stafford, she has altered her Christian beliefs to include extraterrestrials. She insists that all aliens that have been sighted are angels.

On first glance, this theory might seem a little far-fetched, especially in our scientifically oriented age. We could say that it is just a religious crutch, a way of acknowledging the reality of extraterrestrial life without denying the God we have been brought up to accept.

The concept of angels is deeply imbedded in Judeo-Christian theology. In both testaments of the Bible, angels appear as messengers of God and protectors of the godly. Angels have been accepted as real from the beginning, according to biblical scholars.

In the Talmud, the collection of writing constituting the Jewish civil and religious law, it is written that every living thing right down to the smallest blade of grass has its own angel that tells it to grow and progress. Our angel teaches us in the womb, according to the Talmud, every aspect of knowledge possible. When we are born, the angel takes it away and tells us we have the capacity to regain the knowledge, but we must do it by our own initiative.

Under this concept, there are angels for nations as well as individuals. No angel can perform more than one task at any given time, each duty assigned by God, of course. Angels can also appear to whomever they like, whenever they like.

Is it sacrilegious to presume that aliens and angels are one and the same? There is startling evidence, if one looks at the possibility from only one point of view, that they are indeed alternative perceptions of the same phenomenon. It is also intriguing to realize that almost every ancient culture spoke of beings coming down from the heavens. Often they did good things, sometimes they punished, sometimes they flew in objects that resembled extraterrestrial vehicles. Every civilization found by archeologists and historians has had some legend or myth of beings that have descended from the heavens, whether the 'angel-god' Apollo of Greek mythology or the Judeo-Christian Gabriel.

The evidence mounts, according to some of the abductees. As described in the Bible, angels are usually either snow white, gray, or golden and always luminous, traveling in fiery chariots or in clouds that make thunderous noises. In a way, this describes the images of aliens identified by the abductees.

Angels bring messages of peace and good will, as do aliens, according to several abductees. Angels and aliens display healing powers on occasion as Carl Higdon testifies, believing that his health improved overnight, following his encounter with the humanoids. Cherubim, the small angels that travel with God, are mentioned in the Bible as dressing in red. Travis Walton said his aliens were small in stature and garbed in red.

Of course, nonbelievers have reasoned that the sightings of UFOs are a twentieth-century reversion to a primitive need to explain natural phenomena in supernatural terms, and if one takes this view, the recurrence of angels/aliens adds to that argument. It has also been said that UFOs look alike through the ages because of a primeval sameness in human imagination; that is, some archetypal element within us that can create what others have created no matter how removed from their culture we are.

C. G. Jung, the eminent psychologist, wrote in an article, 'Flying Saucers: A Modern Myth of Things Seen in the Skies' (reprinted in *Civilization in Transition*, Bolinger Foundation, 1978):

*Anyone with the requisite historical and psychological knowledge*

> *knows that circular symbols have played an important role in every age; in our own sphere of culture, for instance, they were not only soul symbols but 'God-images'. There is an old saying that 'God is a circle whose center is everywhere and the circumference nowhere.' God in his omniscience, omnipotence and omnipresence is a totality symbol par excellence, something round, complete, and perfect. Epiphanies of this sort are, in the tradition, often associated with fire and light. On the antique level, therefore, the UFOs could easily be conceived as 'gods'. They are impressive manifestations of totality whose simple, round form portrays the archetype of the self, which as we know from experience plays the chief role in uniting apparently irreconcilable opposites.*

For their part, the abductees have compiled listings of evidence that support Jung's thesis. For example, Lydia Stalnaker told us:

'The leader of the aliens on the craft I was on took me before several of the other alien beings and he told me I was born to receive powers from God to help my own kind. I said, "Are you God?" He said, "No." And I said, "Do you know God?" And he said yes they did. So I asked him if they had the same God we have and he replied, "Yes, there is only one God of all the universe." I realized that He's one big God.'

As to those who wonder why Lydia Stalnaker would have been chosen, a woman who at the time of her abduction was a lapsed Christian and divorced, the answer could be said to be in the Bible. Most of the prophets and other holy men and women were people from very humble origins. Stalnaker believed she was given the gift of faith healing, an ability cited in the Bible for several prophets.

Mona Stafford agrees that the aliens she met were angels and that they were working with God. Stafford insists that both she and Elaine Thomas, the third woman captured with Stafford and Louise Smith, felt the presence of God in their contact with the aliens.

'I believe it's of God. I've felt that since the very beginning,' Stafford remembers. 'The first time I was questioned by a newspaper I said that only God could help us from what it was. What I meant was that actually we had to help ourselves because I feel *it is God*. Elaine felt a lot that way, too.'

Faith healer Stalnaker has become a serious student of the Bible since her abduction, and we found her very persuasive. 'The Bible is filled with UFOs,' she insists.

Indeed, virtually every time angels or chariots in the sky are mentioned in the Bible, the resemblance in her eyes to what we, today, call extraterrestrials and UFOs is unmistakable.

For example, the prophet Zechariah had what Stalnaker would say is a more easily identifiable extraterrestrial visitation in the Old Testament. He was approached by a strange man who introduced himself as an angel and showed Zechariah many wondrous things, including a golden seven-armed candelabra (or menorah), as part of an explanation the 'angel' wanted him to grasp about man's future. When Zechariah looked up in the sky above him, he realized that the angel had come from an object which he described as being a 'flying roll' (Zech. 5:1). According to the prophet, the 'roll' was twenty cubits long (about thirty-six feet) and ten cubits high (about eighteen feet).

There were no cigars in ancient Judea, so Zechariah could hardly say he'd seen a cigar-shaped object or vehicle. However, his visual image matches perfectly Betty Hill's initial impression of the UFO that captured her and her husband as 'cigar-shaped.'

Many UFO authorities have described the awesome vehicle that took the prophet Elijah to heaven as a spacecraft. The Bible tells us that Elijah never died; when his time was up, a fiery flying chariot drawn by two fiery horses took him into the sky, presumably to heaven. His student, Elisha, witnessed and described the moment.

Stalnaker has examined the words 'fiery chariot' closely. She insists, as a student of Hebrew, that the actual translation is 'red vehicle.' In fact, according to a Hebrew scholar who asked not to be identified, the word in Hebrew for the chariot would be written in English letters as 'rekevaysh' or, directly translated, 'vehicle with fire' or 'fiery vehicle.'

Numerous modern sightings have been described as fiery or very brightly illuminated flying vehicles. The brilliantly luminous objects seen over the Canal Zone and Panama in 1959, the brilliantly lighted doughnut-shaped craft over Italy in 1978, and the fiery craft that nearly collided with a jet liner en route to Puerto Rico in 1957 are just a few.

As Mona Stafford, herself an artist and familiar with colors and tones, described the vehicle that entrapped her, Louise Smith, and Elaine Thomas in 1976: 'It had the brightest lights I have ever seen. I had never seen colors like it, the red was so beautiful. It was both beautiful and terrifying ... When the lights were on it got very hot as if the lights contained heat. It lit up the area around it like day and more.'

Today, this is considered a UFO. Those fiery chariots, vehicles in which God or His angels are supposed to be riding, are repeatedly described in the Old Testament. God, with fire coming out of His mouth, was seen flying to the defense of the Israelites, at King David's request, in the Book of Samuel (2) and Psalm 18. In Psalm 68, David enumerates the vast number of 'chariots' that are in the biblical air force – 20,000, all manned by angels.

Is this symbolic imagery, or did David really see something fiery (i.e., luminous and glowing) in the sky? Once again, one might wonder why David chose such a vision if it were only an illusion. The scale is far too grand for Lydia Stalnaker to believe it derives from David's talents as a poet. She says, bluntly: 'Where did David come off seeing 20,000 chariots in the sky? And this was a real vision, the nature of the psalm is not makebelieve.'

Stalnaker asks: 'Did you know that angels are flesh and blood? I've been studying the Bible since my abduction. Nowhere in the Bible does it say angels have wings, either. They drink wine, they eat and they ride around in fire chariots. After all, Jacob wrestled with an angel. There must have been something solid for him to grab hold of.'

## DIRECT ENCOUNTERS

Possibly the flying vehicle in the Old Testament most often analyzed by UFO students and the abductees was seen by the prophet Ezekiel. He wrote:

*And I looked, and behold, a whirlwind came out of the north, a great cloud, and a fire unfolding itself, and a brightness was about it, and out of the midst thereof as the colour of amber, out of the midst of the fire . . .*

After describing the beings that emerged from the fiery vehicle, Ezekiel continued:

*Now as I beheld the living creatures, behold one wheel upon the earth by the living creatures, with his four faces. The appearance of the wheels and their work was like unto the color of a beryl: and they four had one likeness: and their appearance and their work was as it were a wheel in the middle of a wheel.*

*When they went, they went upon their four sides: and they turned not when they went. As for their rings, they were so high that they were dreadful; and their rings were full of eyes round about them four. And when the living creatures went, the wheels went by them; and when the living creatures were lifted up from the earth, the wheels were lifted up.*

Ezekiel's vision was no chariot even to conventional biblical scholars. It was a great fiery 'cloud' with a wheel within a wheel that extended from the craft to the earth. Some UFO writers have been inclined to say this was a helicopter, but there is no 'wheel in the middle of a wheel' involved in the mechanics of such a vehicle.

According to the official annotated Hebrew text and English translation of the Old Testament published by the Soncino Press in London, the original Hebrew wording is understood to mean 'one wheel was fixed into another cross-wise, so that in whatever direction the being turned the wheel revolved in that way.' What Ezekiel might have seen, if one subscribes to the angel/alien theory, quite distinctly could have been a stabilizing device, an enormous gyroscope, that balanced the tremendous force of the vehicle's engines while hovering.

Ezekiel's fiery cloud had passengers – each with four faces, one on side side of their heads – a man, a lion, an ox, and an eagle. (These animals each have religious significance unnecessary to elaborate on here.) The beings were further encumbered with four sets of both arms and wings and a single hoof at the bottom of the leg. In addition, they rushed back and forth at lightning speed, glowed brilliantly, and were a burnt-brass color.

Ezekiel also mentioned a roaring noise made by the wheels of the vehicle and the creatures' wings. UFO researchers contend that this is from jet propulsion or jet belts.

In the Book of Revelations, St. John the Divine wrote of having seen figures similar to Ezekiel's, but somewhat simplified, on board the heavenly craft he visited. There, guarding what St. John believed were heavenly elders, stood four beings with eyes in front and in back of their heads. One resembled a man, one a calf, one a lion, and one an eagle, and each had six wings. Other heavenly beings seen on the craft by St. John the Divine included an average-sized man whose skin and hair were white but whose eyes were 'as a flame of fire.' Stalnaker interprets this passage as Ezekiel's beings seen by St. John the Divine in the company of another humanoid that looked remarkably like the glowing-eyed, gray-white space traveler seen by the Hills, Mona Stafford, Travis Walton, and many others. Indeed, since abductees Walton, Stalnaker, and Rolfe reported seeing more than one kind of alien working together, still another similarity is noted.

Believers further emphasize that the aliens the abductees describe as extraterrestrials, the humanlike white (or gray-white) variety, appear as angels throughout the New Testament. (Of course, it could be that angels are white because it is the traditional color of purity.)

In Matthew 28:2, 3, for instance, when Mary Magdalene and Mary, the mother of James, go to visit Christ's grave, they are told by an angel whose 'countenance was like lightning, and his raiment white as snow' that Jesus has left the tomb. Luke (24:4) says there were two angels and describes the beings' garments as 'shining,' the same description Mona Stafford gave to the clothing of the humanoid who visited her six months after her abduction.

Another argument used to compare extraterrestrials of the twentieth century with the biblical angels comes from several chapters in the New Testament (Matt. 17:1-9; Mark 9:2-9) on the transfiguration of Christ.

As Matthew and Mark describe it, Jesus climbed a high mountain with Peter, James, and John. When they reached the summit, a single bright cloud appeared overhead, and some sort of light engulfed Jesus that turned his clothing white and made his face appear to shine. Suddenly, two humanlike figures, identified in the Bible as Moses and Elijah, came down from the 'cloud' and began to speak with Jesus. The three disciples, who could not hear the conversation, became frightened and fell on their knees in prayer. When they again looked up, the beings were gone, and Jesus was alone. He ordered them not to tell anyone what they had seen until he was risen from the dead.

Although even the staunchest believers in the angel/alien theory do not imply that Jesus was an extraterrestrial, he did to a greater extent try to do much the same thing the angels were trying to accomplish: that is, add backbone to a troubled people, to promote peace and good will.

Yet the single cloud that hovered over Jesus on the mountain is much like what we would call a UFO and matches almost identically the single cloud over a field hand in Warwick, England in 1843, according to John Michell and J. M. Rickard's account in *Phenomena; A Book of Wonders*. Three figures he believed to be angels called to him from the cloud, yet no one else saw them. Angels, of course, according to the Talmud, can appear to whomever they like and not to others. Moreover, the brightness of the cloud that hovered over Jesus and his disciples sounds like a luminous vehicle, better known today as a UFO.

Lydia Stalnaker does not find it all that disturbing. She explains that when she is preaching and healing the sick with her new powers, she is often asked where her power came from. 'The aliens told me I was going to get it,' she states calmly. 'But I say it comes from Jesus because He is definitely a part of all this.'

As more evidence that the angels of the Bible and the aliens of today are the same, Stalnaker points to the burning bush on Mount Sinai (Exod. 3:2-4). The verbal retelling of the moment has often left out the fact that when Moses found the burning bush – a vision in which a bush seemed to be in the center of a bright fire that did not consume the foliage – the first thing he saw was an 'angel' stepping out of it. If anyone saw that today, he might say it was an extraterrestrial being stepping out of a glowing aircraft.

On close reading of the Bible, other often neglected passages are found, each ripe for varying interpretations. In the conversion of St. Paul (Acts 22:6-9; 26:13-14), the saint described what some UFO students might say was a UFO.

It is believed that Paul was a leader of the opposition Pharisee group working diligently for a Jewish orthodoxy. One day, as he and some followers were traveling on a lonely stretch of road near Damascus, he was suddenly struck by a beam of extremely bright light out of the sky. According to Paul, the light was 'above the brightness of the sun.' Only Paul was engulfed in the light beam, although his companions could see it. The entire group fell to their knees, and Paul heard a voice, which he took to be Jesus', telling him he had been selected to do a heavenly task.

Travis Walton, as he himself told it, was struck in the chest by a bright light beam (or force field) from the alien craft while his friends fled in fear.

It would appear that whether people who have unusual sightings accept their encounters as being something extraterrestrial, religious, or a fine mix of the two depends on their own predilections. Men of biblical times would naturally explain any phenomenon as a message from God. Naturally, those familiar with space flight in the twentieth century lean toward the extraterrestrial explanation. It is possible, say some of the abductees, to find no contradiction in the two modes of thinking. The latter can even be taken as a confirmation of religious beliefs.

Jessica Rolfe offers her own explanation. Reiterating her belief that the alien races, particularly the *Kuran*, have been among earthlings for thousands of years, she insists that the stories of angels are the human perception of alien visitations.

'Let's take a few premises,' she begins. 'The *Kuran* have tried to be a guiding force on earth, but failed miserably because they don't understand how the human mind works and we don't understand how their minds work. With that, let's take it a step further and say that the burning bush, the angels, all of that are botched attempts by the alien races to help us. Botched not because their messages didn't get across, but because we took them as holy beings and dwelled on that aspect of the "miracle."

'I can't say any more than anyone else if angels from God aren't the aliens, although I personally doubt it. The point is, I think, we should pay more attention to what these supposed angels say. They always give us clues towards leading a better life, the same as the aliens do when we see them today. They want to help us.'

From Lydia Stalnaker's point of view, angels or celestial beings of one form or another have tried to give us verbal guidance, not just for individual improvement – just as her 'voices' told her to become physically fit – but for the good of all human beings.

'Besides the angels,' she says, 'look at the sightings. I believe they are from the same source, and that source is God and these aliens.'

With this as her guideline, Stalnaker would interpret many of the miracle sightings of the nineteenth century as divine in origin but with aliens as the messengers. From Jessica Rolfe's point of view, these miracle sightings would be another 'botched' attempt by the *Kuran* to somehow guide us toward a more harmonic way of life.

One of the more famous sightings mentioned by Stalnaker's adherents occurred in a remote grotto in the French foothills of the Pyrenees Mountains in 1858. Bernadette Soubrious, a teenage student at a school run by the Sisters of Charity in Lourdes, had a vision. While collecting firewood near the grotto, she stopped to wade in the cool brook there when she heard a loud noise. She was frightened, and when the noise began again, she turned toward the front of the grotto, looking for its cause. There was no wind, yet Bernadette noticed immediately that a rosebush at the entrance was blowing about as if there were a strong breeze. Almost simultaneously, she became aware of a gold-colored cloud moving toward her from inside the grotto. A few moments later, a human figure, which the young girl described as a beautiful lady, appeared. The apparition made a friendly gesture to the teenager, and Bernadette got down on her knees and approached the vision. As the devout girl said the rosary, the figure repeated the 'Gloria' with her but nothing else.

After Bernadette had prayed, the 'lady' and the golden cloud returned into the grotto. Her fear gone, Bernadette looked about and realized she had crawled into the brook, but instead of being cold, the water was warm enough for bathing.

Since that time, Lourdes has become a center where the ailing go to seek cures for debilitating illness by the waters.

UFO scholars, who are less prone to 'divine' interpretations, point out that Bernadette would have undoubtedly identified such a luminous, frightening, and unearthly sight to be holy. They say the similarities to UFOs or alien sightings today are undeniable. Even the fact that the water became hot would indicate that the figure and/or the golden cloud that Bernadette saw was probably giving off considerable heat, and the abductees claim that the craft they encountered did precisely that.

Like angels and other heavenly visions, UFOs often vanish

in midair, according to witnesses. The nine seen by Kenneth Arnold did so moments after he first spotted them. *Project Blue Book* contains reports of dozens of UFOs that were on radar or in clear view of pilots one minute and, like the vision at Lourdes, gone the next.

Believers do cite other circumstances that parallel modern UFO encounters. They point to statistics offered by Dr. James Harder of the University of California at Berkeley that 61 percent of the abductees are rural women and 16 percent of them children. Miracle sightings usually happen to members of those two categories.

Devout peasants who know nothing of modern science would be more likely, even today, to label a frightening experience with bright lights and unusual beings godly rather than extraterrestrial. Those who agree with Lydia Stalnaker also point out that the sightings of celestial figures took place long ago. No one would have been looking at that time for aliens from another planet, just as the technological concept of UFOs would not have occurred to Moses and Elisha.


Of all the miracle sightings, the one most often mentioned by believers who claim that aliens and angels are one and the same is the Our Lady of Fatima case of Aljustrel, Portugal.

'If it can be shown conclusively that one such apparition [religious miracle] was the work of saucerians, then it will be senseless to try to explain the others as something different,' writes author R. I. Dione in his book *God Drives a Flying Saucer*. 'The Lady of Fatima incident is a case so immersed in circumstantial evidence of flying saucer origin that even the hardest-nosed skeptic, once familiar with the facts, must concede that saucerians were indeed responsible.'

This most famous vision was seen first in May 1916. While World War I raged throughout Europe, Lucy Abobora and her cousins, Francisco and Jacinta Marta, made a sighting that brought a message of hope and impending peace, according to Msr. William C. McGrath ('The Lady of the

Rosary,' in *A Woman Clothed with the Sun*, John J. Delaney, editor).

The three children, Lucy, Francisco, and Jacinta, were herding sheep outside the village of Aljustrel when suddenly a strong wind shook the trees and a bright white light appeared in the sky. As the ball of light got closer to the children, it took the form of a man, still resplendent with light, who told them he was the 'angel of peace.' The children knelt to pray, and the 'angel' vanished.

The vision of the 'angel' visited the children three separate times over the next few weeks, the last time giving them Holy Communion, or at least giving them a red liquid to drink and a wafer to eat. The children went into such ecstacy that they became physically weak and withdrawn.

Nothing happened for a year, while the war continued to rage around them. Then, on May 13, 1917, in the same spot where they had seen the 'angel' the children saw another apparition. Suddenly, there was a brilliant light, and they saw a figure, which they identified as a woman. The lady shined from head to toe and was absolutely perfect in all respects (much like the humanlike blemishless, handsome 'aliens' seen by Travis Walton or Jessica Rolfe's *Kuran*). The children were mesmerized by the dazzling light and just stared for a long time until the lady told them she was from heaven and asked them to return each month on the thirteenth to see her. The figure made some predictions about the imminent deaths of the two Marta children, which showed clairvoyance not unfamiliar to the so-called extraterrestrials encountered by the abductees, and then vanished.

The children had several more visits from this apparition, most of which were witnessed by the growing throng of faithful who came to believe that the visitor was, in fact, the Heavenly Mother. UFO scholars insist on a close examination of what they actually saw.

On June 13, the visitor came again. It, in all its luminous glory, appeared before the children and told the ten-year-old Lucy to learn to read and write. It stayed for only a few minutes. While the children saw the shining, resplendent lady, all the crowd saw was a singular circular white-gray 'cloud' that hovered over the children.

On July 13, the children were engulfed in a bright light and spoke with the lady, who showed them a vision within a vision, supposedly giving them a look at sinners burning in Hell. In addition, the being attempted to explain to these illiterate peasant children that Russian communism was bad because it enslaved people's minds and made a plea for world peace. Again, the onlookers saw only a cloud and heard a rumble like thunder.

The children did not go to the rendezvous point in August because their parents and the local clergy imprisoned them to prevent the meeting. The awaiting unearthly visitors gave the faithful onlookers quite a show of anger. There were bright light flashes, the sky immediately overhead was turned a sickly yellow color, and the circular cloud appeared out of nowhere to hover over the spot.

On September 13, the children were allowed to return to the meeting place under the watchful eye of their parents, who had to fight their way through the crowd of thousands who were making a pilgrimage to the miracle field. The sky seemed oddly dark as the children reached the little tree where the previous sightings had taken place.

Suddenly, a luminous globe appeared overhead. It moved slowly from east to west above them as a smaller object, a white 'cloud,' came down, and hid the children from the audience. The crowd could only hear Lucy's voice as she spoke with the figure: they could not see anyone. The apparition allegedly again made a plea for peace and told the children a great miracle would take place the following month.

On October 13, the elements seemed against the visitor. It was pouring rain, but that did not stop the thousands of devout onlookers or the bishop and other notables who came to witness the promised miracle.

Again, there was a flash of bright light, the children's faces took on ecstatic expressions, and the crowd assumed they were in the presence of the Virgin Mother. The children saw the lady and watched her extend her hand toward what everyone believed was the sun but could have been a spacecraft or an illusion of some kind since it was cloudy and raining. Rays of light (an energy beam?) extended from the lady's hands to the 'sun.' The being made yet another plea for peace, and the 'miracle' began.

The 'sun' lost its brightness and appeared to become a silver disc-shaped object. Suddenly, multicolored rays of light (laser beams?) shot out of it in every direction. It began spinning madly on its axis and darting around the sky. The 'sun' then rushed toward the crowd, which cried out for mercy and repentance, then just as suddenly returned to its place in the sky and took on its original fire-ball appearance.

The apparition gave Lucy a series of prophecies and a peace plan for ending the war.

Of the predictions Lucy was given, some have come true. One of the predictions, that Russia would return to the ranks of the nonsinners and give up communism, has not happened yet and does not appear likely in the near future. The peace plan Lucy was given was not accepted by the warring parties.

A sealed message was also handed to Lucy by the vision, which was to be opened in 1960. The packet, which was presumed to contain further prophecies, was given to the Roman Catholic church. Rumor has it that Pope John XXIII did open and read it in 1960 but deemed the contents too shocking for the general public. Some speculate that it was a doomsday message or an explanation of what the vision was or a statement that alien beings have been visiting earth since the beginning of time. No one has been told, but all are free to speculate based on their individual preferences.

The abductees and many researchers state that there are undeniable similarities among the physical appearances of angels, heavenly visions, and twentieth-century aliens. All three may have the same purpose, to help heal the sick (Lydia Stalnaker and Lourdes), encourage godliness or ethics, and ask for peace and good will. Today's aliens have never harmed anyone, while they have done the good deeds of angels of the past.

'We correlate all this with a religious experience,' says Dr. James Harder, director of research for APRO. 'Surely, these people, the abductees of the last two decades, have become promoters of world peace and very idealistic.'

One more similarity is striking. In the Fatima sighting, several biblical encounters, and the more recent cases of Mona Stafford, Lydia Stalnaker, and Jessica Rolfe, the celestial beings have insisted that the witness 'learn,' whether reading, lessons of the universe, or karate; the compulsion to learn was a direct result of the experience.

Of course, there are differences that are quite evident as well. Many abductions seem to have no religious function but are more of a biological study of some sort.

Still, UFO scholars insist that we look at the record. Sightings have been made in all civilizations; no culture is without some tradition of supernatural visitors, and all too often the descriptions of the beings and the incidents match. Belief in angels takes religious faith. Belief that aliens are on earth takes a similar fervent faith. There is no proof that either exist. In that way, too, they are alike.

## Chapter Nine

# Where Are They Today?

An old familiar adage tells us that 'you can never go back,' that is, that as time moves ahead, people and things change; we cannot recapture a period of our lives exactly as we remembered it. To try only brings disappointment.

The abductees know how true this is. For although most of them have remained in the same houses and the same communities, their lives and perceptions have changed so much that they can never go back to life as it once was. Whether or not others believe the abductees were captured by aliens, they believe it, and they have been living with that belief, adjusting to it, and sometimes, reordering their priorities because of it.

Many watched helplessly as old friends backed away, unwilling to accept their stories. The witnesses have often had to face months and years of raised eyebrows in the community, of feeling that they are constantly observed under a microscope by their neighbors. The forays cannot be easily forgotten. A wife who left because she could not face the embarrassment of being associated with her husband's encounter is gone forever.

More importantly, the abductees themselves have changed. For whatever really happened to them during the time lapse or during the incident they remember so suddenly, their view of the world and their philosophies of living have been permanently altered.

They have undergone a terribly traumatic period, first facing the reality that they underwent what society regards as a bizarre and possibly psychotic experience, then facing the neighbors, and finally realizing that they must face themselves. They can only ponder what their lives might have been like if this had not happened, if that evening they had taken a wrong turn and been on another road, if somehow it had all happened to someone else. The abductees must cope with their lives as they now are, forever affected by the experience they recall so vividly.

Surprisingly, the majority of the abductees are not sad that they had this experience, not because they have gained financially, because most have not. (Several claim to have actually lost money.) Nor have they enjoyed basking in the spotlight, for there have been positive and negative aspects to their fame.

In reality, the contactees say they appreciate the abduction experience because of how it has changed their outlooks. They told us of having realized that there was more to life than just the mundane mechanics of everyday existence. They have, in fact, found they have gained a new way of looking at their lives, new dimensions worth trying. They read more, think about the meaning of life more, spend more time on leisure activities, work harder on the job, and get more fulfillment from everything. As they describe it, each encounter was almost akin to a religious experience, a fervent revival of faith.

This awakening does not mean they have become preachers of the Gospel by any means. Lydia Stalnaker was a lapsed member of the Church of God before her abduction; now she prays and fasts in the glory of the Almighty and is an evangelist and faith healer. She stands alone, however, the only abductee who has turned to the church. In contrast, Mona Stafford says that before January 6, 1976, going to church every Sunday was one of her priorities. Now she frequently misses Sunday services. Louise Smith was a devout Baptist, a singer with a Gospel choir, but she, too, finds that attending services on Sunday is not absolutely mandatory and can be missed without guilt.

If churchgoing has not increased, most of the abductees have not detected any less belief in God in themselves. Carl Higdon, raised a Baptist but now a Methodist, says he has attended church only twice in five years but insists that the abduction has proved to him more fully that 'God is the supreme being.' Louise Smith adds that 'without the grace of God I never would have made it through this period of my life.'

Whatever their feelings about God and their religions, most of the abductees are delighted in the way their attitudes toward life in general have changed, citing what they see as definite improvements.

Mona Stafford emphasizes that before the experience she was a stern, humorless woman who could never tell a joke or even have a good time. Today she is relaxed. She has learned to accept some kidding, even to joke about herself. If she is late for an appointment or forgets a chore, she feels no guilt. She has learned that there is more to life than a spotless, moral home. There are interesting people, books, knowledge, and much more to explore, she says.

Today, after moving several times, she has settled in Dunnville, Kentucky, where she cares for two boys whose parents died tragically. She is paid by the young wards' relatives and derives much pleasure from her work, turning down more lucrative and prestigious employment because here she feels she is needed and useful, as if she is making a contribution. The boys seem to be thriving.

Stafford's mother and fiancé have passed away, and her relationship with her son may not be the best, but for the first time in her life she feels self-reliant, as if she can control h/ destiny and the quality of her life. At night, she may haunted by memories of her painful abduction, but by da' is more pleasurable than she can ever remember it before.

She has not seen her colleague Louise Smith for some time, but the direction of their lives has been somewhat parallel. Smith enjoys her life in Las Vegas, Nevada, where she has made many friends and lives in a close-knit trailer park. Her hours as the manager of a Mexican restaurant are long, but the work is challenging and suits her outgoing personality. She often muses that she is destined in life to play 'big sister to everyone.'

Like Mona, she leads a quite life, occasionally reading books on the subject of UFOs. She believes that if she had known more about UFOs prior to the abduction, she would have been prepared for the aftermath and perhaps even could have 'learned something from the aliens.' She also fears the aliens may return, that the 'mold' she believes they made of her body will be formed into a human being. She shudders to think what it will be like when she is walking down a street and sees her own image coming her way. Yet she is a survivor.

'I felt alienated for awhile,' she says today, a pensive woman. 'I read more and more about sightings and UFOs today and I can relax. I have come to realize – and those around me have, too – that I am a normal human being and I can survive in whatever I get into. Now if people don't understand, I can understand them. I don't need their support anymore. I have my job, wonderful children and grandchildren, who are always there when I need them. And I have me. That's a lot more than so many others have.'

Travis Walton can match Louise Smith's inner strength, once again a recent acquisition. He lives with his wife Dana and son Clifton in Snowflake, Arizona, not far from his mother. He stays to himself, cuts firewood, and does building repair work to support his family. It is a life he enjoys, one that fits his retiring, private manner. He does not strike observers as the type of person cut out for the public eye, but fate played a trump card in his life.

'I try to keep my experience as a separate part of my life, d people respect that,' he told us. 'I'm still curious and apprehensive about what else happened to me that I can't remember, but I try to live as normally as possible. Surely, the abduction disrupted whatever pattern my life was taking, but who can say where I would be today?'

Carl Higdon is one of the few abductees who can take gentle ribbing from friends about his experience, and he invariably comes across as a mature, decent person. It is no wonder that he has prospered as foreman of an oil rig. He is an able man. He keeps abreast of what is happening to other abductees and even corresponds with a secret woman contactee in Florida. Not prone to conceit, he nevertheless is proud of the way he has handled his experience and the publicity.

'I've always liked doing what I'm doing,' he says, sitting in his comfortable living room. 'Still living in the same house, same town. Doing the things I did before. I've got a better job than I've ever had before, but that's because I work hard, maybe better than most.

'Other people who have had this experience have tried to push it off on other people, make them believe. And me? I have never cared what they had to say. If they don't believe, that's fine. They don't want to talk about it? We don't have to. They usually press me to talk about it. It hasn't helped the other abductees if they've carried on and on about it.'

Of course, Higdon may feel better today because his health has improved; one of the unanswered questions about his experience is that his lungs are now clear of the tuberculosis scars and his gout has disappeared. He has ventured back into the woods to hunt many times. He will do so again.

What will happen to Jeffrey Greenhaw is less clear. Sitting alone in his parents' home in Hartselle, Alabama, he is an unhappy man. He has returned to Alabama after working as a carpenter elsewhere in the South (he will not specify where) and suffers from a back injury that does not seem to heal. Greenhaw confides that he has altered his appearance slightly by adopting a different hair style.

Greenhaw is bitter and disillusioned about America, its government, and its people. He talks of leaving indefinitely, perhaps traveling to Australia, Brazil, New Zealand, or Mexico, four of the many countries to which he has been invited by UFO enthusiasts. 'I'll never try to jam my life down other people's throats,' he insists. 'There are aliens and they'll find out soon enough all those other people who don't believe.'

Betty Hill remains in Portsmouth, New Hampshire, seemingly content with the path her life has taken. She never proselytizes, just shakes off disbelievers as people trying to preserve their own sanity.

Her apartment in Portsmouth, where she has lived for twenty-five years and where she shared her entire married life with Barney, is filled with the memorabilia of fifteen years of UFO involvement. There are pictures of what she believes are UFOs, a large bust on the mantle of the alien she described, and a copy of the book on her abduction, its pages covered with autographs and good wishes penned by the notables she has met doing TV and radio interviews.

She is proud that she was, according to what she has read, probably 'the first woman abducted and Barney may have been the second man,' and she is no doubt more than slightly flattered when it is suggested that someday the Hills, as the first publicized abductees, may find that their names are known to school children everywhere. Her involvement with UFO research is also a means of keeping Barney alive, for she speaks of him with love and laughter while punctuating her own adventures since his death in 1969.

'I would say that the only difference this has meant is that, while everyone knew us locally and many statewide, we are now known worldwide,' Betty says, uttering what is doubtlessly a true statement considering their community and political work both before and after the incident. 'I'm a retired social worker now, I retired as a supervisor, but I'm not counseling people in UFOs. If you don't believe, that's your protection. I feel good.'

## WHERE ARE THEY TODAY?

The two women most affected by their new-found psi awareness, Ellecia Gruen and Lydia Stalnaker, seem to have more enthusiasm for living than ever before. For Gruen, every day is a challenge as she discovers new psi 'lessons,' as she calls them, and pursues her many hobbies. An active woman, she says that the period of 1976 when the UFOs were flying above her house was 'the only time in my life when I didn't do diddley.'

The 'UFO Lady of Ogden Center' is separated from her husband now, partly because he wanted her to gain financially from her abilities. She is unperturbed about being alone and is glad that her children have a keen interest in what she does. Friends say she is the same Ellecia they knew years ago.

Perhaps, Gruen herself claims, 'I judge people less since this, but I've always been weird for around here. I've always had a mind of my own, done what I've wanted to do. Other people don't sway my ideas. If I feel something is right to do, I do it.

'I just say that I don't and won't live other people's lives. I don't expect them to live mine. So maybe I've been a bit weird or different, but I'm not crazy.'

Gruen might be respected for many reasons besides her public stance. Here is a woman, raised in an orphanage, married, who has always been independent and strong. Gruen has dared to be a nonconformist in a small Midwestern town. Her neighbors have continued to support her. That in itself stands as testimony to her contribution to her community.

Like Gruen, Lydia Stalnaker has an upbeat view of the world. She was an introverted, unhappy woman prior to the abduction; now she is remarried, has a purpose in life, and is traveling and exploring worlds she never knew existed. Whether she was chosen for this role by the aliens 'because of my chemistry,' as she has said, is speculative. Still, there is no denying that her work as a faith healer and evangelist has brought hope and comfort to many who believe in her.

'I want to be a better evangelist,' she told us. 'I guess I'm doing the work I was chosen for. I don't worry about other people. I have my work now. I feel needed, I feel like I have a purpose in life. If someone doesn't believe, they don't come near me. I can't beat them until they believe in UFOs. You can't force them. All I know is that the aliens made my life a whole lot better.'

Jessica Rolfe lives in Los Angeles, California, where she pursues her joint acting-writing career and also works as an agent's assistant, aiding writers and actors in their careers. Although she has no plans to write a book on her story, she is working on a UFO documentary film. Her experience is shared only with those who probe and who she feels have enough prior knowledge on the subject to understand what she is about to tell. One must first demonstrate that he has information the average person does not have before he is ready, in her eyes, to hear more.

'I have no idea why I am the way I am,' she says in her usual quiet and intense manner. 'I think sometimes that it's destiny that I meet the people that I confide in. It's like the *Kuran* want me to remember where I've been and where I'm going. I feel different, but not special because of what has happened to me. There is no need to capitalize on it, since the knowledge I have seems gift enough.'

There is no question in Rolfe's mind that her abductions and encounters were worthwhile. She is glad that it happened to her. Her fellow abductees, while they all seem at least somewhat better for it, do not always agree. Still, their outlook has been altered permanently; they speak of having gone from living a mundane existence to a life rich and full.

'I'm better for all this, I guess,' Travis Walton offers, perhaps speaking for more than himself. 'I used to have my head to the ground; now I know there is more to what's here. The universe is bigger, more immense, more spectacular than I ever imagined. But what a price I have paid for that broadening of my horizons. I'm a better person, but on a day-to-day basis it is more difficult to live.'

## WHERE ARE THEY TODAY?

There is a song about two groups of people, one who lived inside a castle and the other who lived outside the walls. The people inside the walls were thought by those outside to have all the riches of the world. They seemed happy, joyful, and content, while the outsiders worked hard and were grumpy, dull, and tired.

One day, the outsiders became consumed with jealousy of the others' life style and stormed the castle, tearing down the walls and killing many of the happy inside dwellers. They demanded to see the source of the wealth and exuberance and were told that the riches were underneath a rock. When they lifted the rock, they saw three words, 'Peace on Earth.' The abductees seem to concur that belief in harmony and the overwhelming will to live your life accordingly leads to true wealth.

The abduction experience is akin to being an outsider who was allowed inside the walls of the castle, and, once inside, found no hostility, just a message for peace. Whatever the individual experience may have been, every abductee seems to have found an inner tranquility that is tested not only by their actions or anxiety but also by the rest of us, whom they would call outsiders. It is almost as if they have learned a secret that cannot be explained by words.

'I always say that I wish this had never happened to me because of the mental stress,' Louise Smith claims. 'Sure, I live in fear that the aliens have made a mold of me and that I'll walk down the street and see myself coming from the other direction.

'But then I look at myself and I feel better inside. I think my real regret is that I didn't find the aliens' secret. Maybe they are just playing with us abductees, but I know they can help us and I don't mean by coming down and giving lessons on a blackboard. I mean we can be helped by knowing that we can do better.'

Jessica Rolfe would agree. 'They have tried to make themselves known to us, but it never works out,' she told us. 'They don't understand us any more than we understand them. If they came to us today we'd probably want to make them our leaders, but I don't think they want that. They can show us what harmony is. They want us to understand the scheme. The abductions are just their way of having fun. I guess we should be flattered that they really do find us amazing in our own way.'

Mona Stafford and Lydia Stalnaker also speak of a better world that could be ours if we would accept the aliens and believe in them. However, both take a much more fatalistic view of the situation than the other abductees. Stafford and Stalnaker are sure there will be a judgment day, but that appears to come more in their perception of the aliens than in what was said to them.

Stafford is convinced that the aliens will reveal themselves to the entire world soon. When that happens, she confides, 'We will go to war with them, that is, most people will. But they will all be killed while those who believe and do not try to fight them will be helped. Everything will be better afterwards.'

One of the reasons Stafford is always ready to tell her story to reporters is that she feels this message of belief is vitally important for everyone to hear. 'It's the most important thing there is,' she insists.

Betty Hill is not prepared to go as far as Stafford and Stalnaker in predicting an alien takeover. She does believe that if the aliens decide to dominate the earth, humans will not have much of a chance repulsing them. However, she does not fret over the possibilities. 'You can't have nightmares over this,' she soothes her listeners. 'You can't worry about it. If they are intelligent enough to have created space ships and travel throughout the galaxy, then they can come and go and do with us as they please. We can't devise any contingency plans.'

Whatever the impressions of the aliens' aims toward humanity, each of the abductees has developed an intense interest in discovering more about the aliens, who they are and how they travel. Their initial reactions were to look up in the sky whenever they were outdoors at night, hoping to see another craft. Travis Walton admits that he carried a camera around with him for quite some time after his abduction. He once took a picture of an odd-looking object in the sky, which he later learned was actually a weather balloon.

Jeffrey Greenhaw has not been discouraged by his sad experiences since the encounter and boasts that he has collected enough UFO reading material to last a lifetime. He has remained in contact with several independent UFO groups around the world and claims to have seen UFOs in the sky over Alabama in recent years but declines to discuss them for fear of additional ridicule.

Carl Higdon, Louise Smith, and Mona Stafford pore through newspaper and magazine articles and books on the subject whenever they can. All three are exceptionally interested in finding out what similarities exist among the abductees and their experiences. It is as if they are still searching for some reason for their own capture and some confirmation that others have gone through the same draining experience.

Most of the abductees wonder who the aliens really are and why they bothered to capture and examine these particular humans.

Several evenings each week, Betty Hill travels from her home to an open field sixteen miles southwest of Portsmouth that she has come to refer to as 'my area, I call it that to give it a name.' On these evenings, she eats a leisurely dinner at a nearby restaurant, then marches into the field with her dog Brandy, always with her eyes on the sky. Betty feels she has indentified the sky above this spot as a UFO meeting place or an area where the aliens have flight patterns. She frequently does see low-flying wingless craft overhead, she claims.

Hill usually greets the UFOs with a warm wave and the words 'Hello, friends.' She has never received an answer, but she feels that the photographs she has taken are accurate. Her research has given her life greater meaning, and she now is pleased that she was abducted.

She criticizes other researchers by saying, 'They're doing it backwards. They talk to the witnesses and try to learn that way. I investigate the UFOs.'

'In my area they seem to come from all directions,' Betty told us. 'They have a pattern like the spokes of a wheel that come to a hub. They spread out and go in different directions. You can speculate that they're getting their orders for the night. I don't know how many places they're coming from, but they're all together. And its the same UFOs that are coming back night after night.'

She does not believe that the aliens are living on the craft that she sees, but that her UFOs are travelers from a mother ship of some sort. She has taken reporters and other investigators into this area on occasion but only if they promise to write precisely what they have seen and nothing else.

Hill remains unaware that Jessica Rolfe has also located an area in New Hampshire where she, too, has traveled many times in order to spot UFOs. While living in Boston, Massachusetts, Rolfe often took her friends to an area near Pierce Bridge, New Hampshire, where she says sightings were frequent.

'I was on radio for many years talking about my sightings and other abductions,' she recalls. 'I used a pseudonym on the radio show, I just can't see a reason to reveal my identity yet.

'Our sightings in New England were frequent. It was also possible to make telepathic contact with some of the alien races. This may be hard for some to fathom, but they really do come here because we are fascinating. Our race, our planet and our solar system – it all is unusual to them. There is nothing like it.'

Through her communications with the aliens, Rolfe has developed a theory of the visitations based on the history of creation she claims the aliens told her. Because human beings migrated from another planet to Earth, the natural evolution of this planet was interrupted, and now there is conflict between planets.

Rolfe believes we are the only race to have created the concept of war and of boundaries. We have more children than other races, we use complex written and spoken languages, and we have an immense variety of cultures. We also have ethnic polarization, and since reincarnation is, she contends, a fact, we are the only race to have experienced the phenomenon of ghosts.

Rolfe realizes her research reveals information that challenges basic anthropological science, and religious beliefs, one of the reasons she finds it best to remain a secret abductee.

Mona Stafford, who, like the others, has found that people seek her out with their information about sightings, has become increasingly interested in reports of Big Foot, the Sasquatch, roaming the woods of Kentucky. The encounters fascinate her, and she eagerly absorbs all evidence that the creatures exist. Jessica Rolfe says that she has been told by the aliens that the so-called 'Big Foot' is another alien race that stumbled upon earth but was driven to remote corners by the stronger and more populous human beings.

Most of the abductees are convinced that a tremendous number of people have seen UFOs but simply don't realize it. A 1973 Gallup poll reported that 11 percent of Americans admitted to having seen something in the sky they would categorize as a UFO; the percentage may be higher now.

'Most people have seen a UFO,' Betty Hill insists. 'I've come to believe that. They just don't tell other people. I am more convinced than ever that there is life on other planets. The UFOs do things that nothing on this earth can duplicate. I had a stain on my dress after capture and no chemist has ever been able to tell me what the substance is. I have seen UFOs camouflage themselves as barns and farmhouses. The evidence is just too strong.'

Like the others, she is also convinced that it is just a matter of time before the aliens make themselves known, but she sadly contemplates what we would do if the aliens said. 'Take us to your leaders.' 'Who are the leaders today?' she asks.

Even those with multiple abduction experiences offer no suggestions to the person so titillated by the prospect of an encounter that he asks, 'How can it happen to me?' Human beings are not yet in control of these contacts, that is for sure. Betty Hill cautions interested parties to keep away from alien craft if they should land. She adds that if one faces an abduction, he should go willingly, without a struggle.

Jessica Rolfe scoffs at her advice. She insists that there is nothing to be frightened of, that the aliens have no concept of war, murder, malicious attacks, or any other such human instincts. 'If you have an encounter, just relax, be friendly,' she advises. 'If you want to speak with them, you can't be frightened, can't send out negative vibrations or they will back away.'

Whether or not they are involved in research, the abductees usually find themselves in a singular position. Their situation is not unlike that of a minority family in a small town or the American who travels abroad although he does not speak any language but English. In both cases, there is a distinct feeling of separation from those around them.

A small group cannot sway a nation's beliefs, and the abductees have not made an effort to try. They experience the same ups and downs as the rest of us in the workaday world. Yet there is a difference. They have been involved in something rare, and they have a vision of a broader universe: a larger world than the rest of us perceive. Perhaps we should investigate.

# Conclusion

When we were interviewing the abductees and doing the research necessary for this book, the question we were most frequently asked by friends and acquaintances was, 'Well, *do* you believe in UFOs?' It was easy to say we did, indeed, believe in UFOs since, by the strictest definition, an unidentified flying object could be a sponge thrown into the air by a neighbor. If a distant viewer cannot say precisely what it is, then it becomes an unidentified flying object. Similarly, there have been thousands of pictures taken of objects suspended in the sky that can't be readily identified. They could be craft used by alien races, they could be weather balloons, they could even be some sort of unusual natural phenomenon.

The abductees force us to reckon with a far more intense question. We are being asked to speculate whether the earth is being visited by humanoid races from other planets and other solar systems. It is even possible, if we agree with statements made by Jessica Rolfe, Lydia Stalnaker, and Carl Higdon, among others, that the aliens are already living among us, hidden from conventional view.

The abductees we interviewed all appear to be rational, and even if their explanations and evidence are not entirely adequate, neither is the material used to discredit them. Most often, the skeptics have implied that the abductees are experiencing some kind of delusion. Yet professionals, both believers and skeptics, who have examined them say no. It seems doubtful that they are perpetrating a hoax since they have had problems in their communities and not one of them has attempted to 'cash in' on the experience. Very few abductees went out of their way to see their name in print; not one actively sought publicity – the reporters came to them, often in droves.

It has been theorized that the abductees are experiencing the effects of a hypnogogic state, when vivid and amorphous mental images of whirling balls and geometric forms and black and fiery shapes appear before us during times of fatigue and drowsiness. Could both of the Hills, the three women from Kentucky, and the seven men in the truck in Arizona have experienced the same hypnogogic phenomena simultaneously?

Even if we hypothesize that Travis Walton is deluded, what about the other six men who claim to have seen the craft and the beginning of the abduction? It is highly doubtful they all conspired to concoct the story, especially when the foreman of the crew – to whom time was money – was the loudest of Walton's defenders and eventually did the illustrations for Walton's book. It is also absurd to insist that Louise Smith, Mona Stafford, and Elaine Thomas concocted their story and were able individually to draw a practically identical picture of the craft. There is just no motivation for this.

Still there is only the word of each abductee, that is, if we don't accept Jeffrey Greenhaw's four pictures as genuine. As to the birth of psi awareness in some of the contactees, it seems obvious that if someone does not believe in extraterrestrials, he is not going to believe in the origins of the new-found powers of the abductees, either. One California psychiatrist told us, 'I believe that we may have been, are being or will be visited by alien races, but it has not been proven to me. As for psi awareness, I believe it is a possibility, but I don't really believe it has been proven to the naked eye, let alone passed the scrutiny of science.' One wonders if anything besides personal experiences would constitute proof.

Should we leave final interpretations to scientists and historians? Despite their fine records, they have not always been infallible. For example, while there are many theories of the creation of the universe, such as the Big Bang theory, none

## CONCLUSION

allows for the story of creation told in Genesis, but this has not led churchgoers to disregard the Bible.

Similarly, there may very well be neither UFOs nor alien races but not because scientists have never seen them. Like a belief in an omnipotent creator, belief in extraterrestrial life is a matter of faith.

The track record of scientists has not always been perfect. In the 1600s, Giordano Bruno, the Italian astronomer, and many others were burned at the stake in Europe for claiming that the Earth revolved around the sun. Galileo had to face the Inquisition on many occasions, knowing that his discoveries were correct, because the church was sure he was performing some satanic deeds and the 'scientific' institutions were not yet ready for his genius.

If Betty Hill, Jessica Rolfe et al, cannot prove beyond a reasonable doubt that there were visits from alien races, neither can a scientist prove that there have not been.

People now are considered more sophisticated than those of yesteryear. We no longer are frightened by eclipses or other such natural events. Abductees and UFO witnesses would insist that they know the difference between the solid metal craft they believe they saw and some freak of nature in the sky.

The need to compile alternate theories about what the abductees did see is in a sense understandable. If we believe in UFOs and accept the possibility of alien visits, there remains a level at which we cannot fathom these visits because we still have not seen them ourselves.

As we were writing this book, we, like every other writer who has tackled the subject of UFOs, tried to find alternative explanations for what the abductees had seen. After spending many hours dreaming up often absurd scenarios, it suddenly hit us that we were being incredibly arrogant. There is nothing wrong with conjuring up half a dozen possible explanations except that it puts us in the position of saying somehow our reasoning is more logical than the perception of others. We had to remind ourselves that we were not on the scene at the time of the sightings and abductions. We have no right to tell the abductees what they saw, although we have every right to question the reality of the vision. No matter how much information they may have given us about their experiences or how educated in the sciences we may be, we were not there – on a quiet highway in New Hampshire or a forest in Wyoming. We did not see what they saw or feel what they felt.

Certainly, we can poke holes in each of their stories, but the evidence for the alternatives is just as weak. For example, one UFO investigator has repeatedly written that Betty and Barney Hill observed the imposing view of Jupiter often seen in the sky rather than a craft. There is no evidence, however, that Jupiter was visible that September night in 1961.

Once again, we can only speculate on what most people would do if confronted with extraterrestrial space travelers. Would we be instantly friendly or pull out the old shotgun and fight for our lives without giving the visitors a chance to explain themselves? In 1938, Orson Wells's 'War of the Worlds' radio broadcast of a fictional alien invasion frightened people so that they sat on their porches with their rifles. One man in New Jersey became so confused that he riddled a windmill with bullets, convinced that it was a landing Martian craft. Who knows what he would have done had a real craft been hovering overhead.

Many years may pass before people know beyond a reasonable doubt if there are alien races in the galaxy. Someday, having scanned every planet, we may realize that we are, indeed, all alone, that UFOs and the *Kuran* were all a mirage. Or mankind could find the aliens standing among us, shaming us into seeing the conditions we have created for ourselves on our earth.

We do not know if there really are alien races. However, the concept of extraterrestrials is doing mankind no harm and could potentially be helpful. All the abductees we interviewed have a better outlook on life. If people who come in contact with either real or imagined aliens become psychic, and this ability is helpful to us all, why complain?

# Bibliography

## BOOKS

Bowen, Charles, ed. *The Humanoids.*
   Chicago: Henry Regnery, Inc., 1969.
Delaney, John J., ed. *A Woman Clothed with the Sun.*
   New York: Image Books, 1961.
Dione, R. I. *God Drives a Flying Saucer.*
   New York: Bantam Books, 1973.
Flammonde, Paris. *UFOs Exist!*
   New York: G. P. Putman, 1976.
Fuller, John G. *The Interrupted Journey.*
   New York: Berkley Medallion Books, 1974.
Hertz, Dr. J. H., ed. *The Pentateuch and Haftorahs.*
   London: Soncino Press, 1960.
Jung, Dr. Carl Gustav. *Civilization in Transition.*
   vol. 10 (collected works). New York: Bollinger Foundation, 1978.
Michell, John and J. M. Rickard. *Phenomena; A Book of Wonders.*
   New York: Pantheon Books, 1977.
Soule, Gardner. *UFOs and IFOs: A Factual Report on Flying Saucers.*
   New York: G. P. Putman, 1967.
Steiger, Brad, ed. *Project Blue Book.*
   New York: Ballantine Books, 1976.
Von Daniken, Erich. *Chariots of the Gods,*
   New York: Bantam Books, 1971.
Walton, Travis. *The Walton Experience.*
   New York: Berkley Medallion Books, 1978.

## ARTICLES

'A Town in Texas Ponders Mystery of 1897 Spaceman.'
   *New York Times*, February 26, 1979.
'Air Mystery in Paris.' *New York Times*, February 22, 1956.

## DIRECT ENCOUNTERS

'Airliner Avoids Flaming Object.' *New York Times*, March 10, 1957.
'Ancient Flying Saucer.' *New York Times*, February 25, 1954.
Bommersbach, Jana. 'U.F.O.s Are Real, He Says—Just Ask the C.I.A. for Proof.' *US*, March 6, 1979.
'Bright Flying Disk Reported in Jersey.'
 *New York Times*, January 14, 1966.
Browne, Malcolm W. 'U.F.O.s Add Spice to Life of Latins.'
 *New York Times*, July 14, 1968.
'Canada to Study Flying Saucers.' *New York Times*, November 12, 1953.
'C.I.A. Papers Detail U.F.O. Surveillance.'
 *New York Times*, January 13, 1979.
'Cups or Saucers?' *Time*, September 1957.
'Excerpts From Case Histories Appearing in Colorado Report on U.F.O.s' *New York Times*, January 10, 1969.
'Flying Object Puzzles Panama.' *New York Times*, January 25, 1959.
'Flying Objects Seen in Argentina.' *New York Times*, June 3, 1962.
'Flying Saucer Spotted.' *New York Times*, September 19, 1959.
'40 in Michigan Report Mysterious Flying Objects.'
 *New York Times*, March 22, 1966.
'Hunt Pilot Who Called in U.F.O.'
 *New York Daily Press*, October 25, 1978.
'Incident at Falkville.' *UFO Diary*, March 1978.
'It's the Flying Saucer Season Again; Sphere is One of Those Things.'
 *World Telegram and Sun*, May 23, 1955.
Kilgallen, Dorothy. 'EEEK!—From Space.'
 *Journal American*, May 22, 1955.
Lyons, Richard D. 'Air Force Closes Study of U.F.O.s'
 *New York Times*, December 18, 1969.
'Martians Over France.' *Time*, October 25, 1954.
'Moon Flight Reported.' *New York Times*, November 26, 1957.
Oberg, James, 'UFO Update: Betty Hill.' *Omni*, December 1978.
Riding, Alan, 'Scientists and Laymen in Conflict at World Conference of U.F.O.s.' *New York Times*, April 25, 1977.
 'U.F.O. Buffs Want U.S. Help.' *New York Times*, April 21, 1977.
Rugaber, Walter. 'Flying Objects are Called Gas.'
 *New York Times*, March 26, 1966.
Satchell Michael. 'UFOs Vs. USAF.'
 *Parade Magazine*, December 10, 1978.
'Soviet Study of U.F.O.s Is Reported Under Way.'

## BIBLIOGRAPHY

*New York Times*, November 12, 1967.
Sullivan, Walter. 'Soviet U.F.O. Plan Has Familiar Ring.'
   *New York Times*, December 10, 1967.
'U.F.O. Verdict: Believers Find It Unbelievable.'
   *New York Times*, January 12, 1969.
'Strange Radio Pulses Reported by Moscow.'
   *New York Times*, July 17, 1973.
'3 Aides Selected in Saucer Inquiry.'
   *New York Times*, October 8, 1966.
'Some U.F.O. Cases Are Unexplained.'
   *New York Times*, January 10, 1969.
Talbert, Ansel E. 'Air Force to Probe New "Flying Saucers" over Europe.' *New York Herald Tribune*, December 10, 1954.
Tanner, Henry. 'Italian Skies Peppered by Lighted Doughnuts— Some Say U.F.O.s.' *New York Times*, December 17, 1978.
Teltsch, Kathleen. 'U.N. Hears Call to Debate U.F.O.s.'
   *New York Times*, October 8, 1977.
'UFOs Sighted at Bases, Defense Chiefs Report.'
   *Detroit News*, January 19, 1979.
'U.N. Urged to Set Up an Agency for U.F.O.'
   *New York Times*, November 29, 1977.

# ALSO AVAILABLE IN CORONET BOOKS

**LYALL WATSON**
- ☐ 18833 2 Supernature — £1.50
- ☐ 24856 4 Lifetide — £1.50
- ☐ 19989 X The Romeo Error — £1.25
- ☐ 21974 2 Gifts of Unknown Things — £1.25

**BILL SCHUL and ED PETTIT**
- ☐ 21012 5 The Secret Power of Pyramids — 95p
- ☐ 21815 0 The Psychic Power of Pyramids — 95p

**CARL SAGAN**
- ☐ 25348 7 Broca's Brain — £1.50

**ADRIAN BERRY**
- ☐ 19924 5 The Next Ten Thousand Years — £1.00

**LEN ORTZEN**
- ☐ 24263 9 Strange Stories of UFO's — 95p

*All these books are available at your local bookshop or newsagent, or can be ordered direct from the publisher. Just tick the titles you want and fill in the form below.*

Prices and availability subject to change without notice.

---

CORONET BOOKS, P.O. Box 11, Falmouth, Cornwall.

Please send cheque or postal order, and allow the following for postage and packing:

U.K. – 40p for one book, plus 18p for the second book, and 13p for each additional book ordered up to a £1.49 maximum.

B.F.P.O. and EIRE – 40p for the first book, plus 18p for the second book, and 13p per copy of the next 7 books, 7p per book thereafter.

OTHER OVERSEAS CUSTOMERS – 60p for the first book, plus 18p per copy for each additional book.

Name .................................................................................................

Address ..............................................................................................

..........................................................................................................